Every Day
with J...

The Visio...

'Blessed is the one who reads the words of this
prophecy, and blessed are those who hear it and
take to heart what is written in it ...''
Revelation 1:3

Selwyn Hughes
Revised and updated by Mick Brooks
FURTHER STUDY: IAN SEWTER

© CWR 2013. Dated text previously published as *Every Day
with Jesus: The Final Word* (May/June 1999) by CWR. This
edition revised and updated for 2013 by Mick Brooks.

Selwyn Hughes wished to acknowledge the help he received from the following
works in compiling this issue of *Every Day with Jesus: Reversed Thunder* by Eugene
H. Peterson (HarperSanFrancisco, 1991) and *The Message of Revelation: I Saw
Heaven Opened* by Michael Wilcox (IVP, 1991).

CWR, Waverley Abbey House, Waverley Lane, Farnham, Surrey GU9 8EP, UK
Tel: 01252 784700 Email: mail@cwr.org.uk
Registered Charity No. 294387. Registered Limited Company No. 1990308.

Unless otherwise stated, all Scripture quotations are from the Holy Bible,
New International Version. © International Bible Society.

Cover image: getty/Dimitri Vervitsiotis
Quiet Time image: fotosearch
Printed in England by Linney Print

CWR

MIX
Paper from
responsible sources
FSC® C015900
www.fsc.org

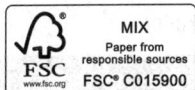

Every Day with Jesus is available in **large print** from CWR. It is also available on **audio and DAISY**
in the UK and Eire for the sole use of those with a visual impairment worse than N12, or who are
registered blind. For details please contact **Torch Trust for the Blind**, Tel: 01858 438260.
Torch Trust for the Blind, Torch House, Torch Way, Northampton Road, Market Harborough LE16 9HL.

A word of introduction ...

Frequently, people used to write to Selwyn asking him to prepare a series of meditations on one of the most confusing books of the Bible - Revelation. He resisted for some time because of the controversy which surrounds the book. Sadly, some friends and church communities have been known to part company because of disputes over the interpretation of John's vision. So, it was with considerable caution and prayer that Selwyn set out to pen these devotions.

Selwyn chose to write, not following a particular school of thought, but focusing on the themes and overall message of the book, applying them devotionally. Over the years, this is something I too have learned to do when grappling with seemingly confusing passages of Scripture; to pause and ask God: What is the purpose behind this passage? What do You want me to learn? How can this help me to live my life for You?

In this issue, Selwyn focuses on central truths and narratives and applies them in a way which will fill you, not with end-time worries and angst, but with joy - hopefully putting a spring in your step as you go out into the day, secure in the knowledge that the One True God, our good Father in heaven, goes with you.

Revelation comes with a promise of blessing for those who read its pages. So, I pray that as you journey through this issue, you will discover that blessing, and that God will 'fill you with the knowledge of his will through all spiritual wisdom and understanding' (Col. 1:9).

Sincerely yours, in His name

Mick

Mick Brooks, Consulting Editor

Free small-group resources to accompany this issue can be found at www.cwr.org.uk/extra. The EDWJ Facebook community is growing! To join the conversation visit www.facebook.com/edwjpage

MAY/JUN
2013

Every Day
with Jesus

The Vision

'Blessed is the one who
reads the words of this
prophecy, and blessed
are those who hear it
and take to heart what
is written in it ...'
Revelation 1:3

Be revived and refreshed by God's Word

CWR

Quiet Time

Through the world's mounting
problems, pain and perversity
God speaks again to His people,
 'No matter what happens
  keep the faith.
   Keep watching and waiting.
   Keep your eyes on Me.
    Keep telling My truth.
     Keep living My love.
       Keep remembering that
  before the foundation of the world
  I already spoke the Final Word.
  His name is Jesus.'
He is coming again
with shouts of victory!

Susan Lenzkes © 2012

A book for today

FOR READING & MEDITATION – REVELATION 1:1-2

'The revelation of Jesus Christ, which God gave him to show
his servants what must soon take place.' (v.1)

During different periods of history, different books of
the Bible have come into prominence. St Augustine,
for example, looking for the city of God amid the rubble
of the decaying Roman Empire, turned to Genesis. Martin
Luther, bent on expounding the doctrine of justification by
faith, focused on the book of Romans. *The book for today, I
believe, is the book of Revelation.*

However, several thoughts must engage our attention
as we begin. Revelation is a prophecy about things *soon*
to take place. The Greek word here translated 'soon'
is *tacheos*, which also means 'quickly'. Our
English word 'taxi' best gives the flavour of the
Greek word (even though there is no linguistic
connection). When we shout 'Taxi!' there is a
sense of immediacy, of needing to get somewhere
quickly, especially if there is an emergency.

The book is not the revelation *of* John but the
revelation of Jesus *to* John. The primary purpose
of the book is not to provide us with a timetable
for the future; it's a revelation of the living,
majestic, conquering Christ. Is not this precisely
what the Church needs at this time – a vision of
the transcendent, preeminent rule of Jesus our
Saviour? The people of God, set as we are in the midst
of a hostile environment, need to dwell on the fact that
Jesus is *Lord*. 'A Church with its back to the wall fighting
for survival,' said John Stott, *'must see Christ.'* Notice the
words, 'The revelation of Jesus Christ, *which God gave him.'*
Elsewhere in the New Testament it is Jesus who reveals
God; here the roles are reversed. Now God is revealing
Jesus. Can anything be more awesome than to see Jesus
'uncovered' in all His glory?

FURTHER STUDY

Matt. 17:1-8;
Rev. 1:17

1. How did
the disciples
respond to
spiritual
revelation?

2. How should
we respond?

**My Father and my God, may I be open to all that You want to
show me of Your Son, for although I know Him, there is so much
more of Him to know. Reveal more of Him to me in the days that
lie ahead, dear Father. In Jesus' name. Amen.**

The message

FOR READING & MEDITATION – REVELATION 1:3

'Blessed is the one who reads the words of this prophecy,
and blessed are those who ... take [it] to heart ...' (v.3)

A special blessing, we are told, awaits those who read or hear words of the book of Revelation and 'take to heart what is written in it'. Our text indicates that the book was not only to be read by individuals, but also meant to be read aloud in the churches. The immediate aim of Revelation was to encourage Christians suffering for their faith, so that they could face the difficult days that lay ahead. That is not to say it does not have a message for us today (indeed, it deals with much that still lies ahead). However, a primary purpose was to support the persecuted Christians of that time by revealing that though evil would be allowed to continue, nothing would be allowed to thwart God's eternal purposes. *This was the message that was to be taken to heart.*

FURTHER STUDY

Josh. 1:1-9;
Psa. 1:1-6

1. How can we take Scripture to heart?

2. Contrast the wicked and the righteous.

Unfortunately many approach the book of Revelation for no other reason than to find keys to unlock the future. Will the Church go through the tribulation? Is there to be a millennium of peace on the earth? How will everything come about? These are interesting questions, of course, but they are not the first questions to be asked of Revelation. The most significant questions are these: Is Jesus Lord of the universe? Are all things proceeding according to plan – the divine plan? Is there an horizon to history? And the answer is a resounding 'Yes'. Of more importance than establishing a particular theory of Revelation is that we grasp its underlying message, namely that Jesus Christ has control of the universe, and that when ultimately all is revealed, history will prove to be *His* story. Believe me, when we catch a glimpse of the grand design on the right side of the tapestry we can face anything. Anything!

O my Father, please help me for it is so easy to miss the wood for the trees. Save me from becoming so interested in the symbols in this book that I lose sight of the Saviour and fail to take its underlying message to my heart. Amen.

The magnificent Christ

FOR READING & MEDITATION - REVELATION 1:4-5

'John, To the seven churches in the province of Asia:
Grace and peace to you ...' (v.4)

The book of Revelation contains a number of great themes, the first being the glory and magnificence of Jesus. While in one sense the whole book unfolds this theme, it finds a powerful focus in this first chapter. John is instructed by an angel to write to the seven churches in Asia, and he opens with a greeting found in many of the New Testament letters, namely 'Grace and peace to you ...' 'Grace and peace' you will observe, not 'Perplexity and puzzlement'!

Notice, however, that John's greeting is not from himself but from the triune God. How amazing to be greeted by the Trinity! First, the Father, 'who is, and who was, and who is to come'. Next, the Holy Spirit, as expressed by the term 'the seven spirits before his throne'. But isn't the Spirit one, and not seven? Archbishop Trench provided a helpful explanation for this. 'The Holy Spirit,' he wrote, 'is being depicted here not so much in His personal unity as His manifold energies. Though the Spirit is indeed one, He ministers to each of the seven churches at one and the same time.'

But it is Jesus Himself who is given the fullest description, and is presented to us first as 'the faithful witness' – the One who during His ministry here on earth never failed to present God's truth. Next, He is called 'the firstborn from the dead', meaning that He is the first of an order which others can follow. John's final description of Jesus is that of 'ruler of the kings of the earth'. A Christian community facing uncertainty, ostracism, and perhaps even persecution, will do well to remember that kings and rulers, though they may not realise it, are themselves being ruled. Our Lord is for ever the King of kings.

FURTHER STUDY

Isa. 11:1-2;
Matt. 26:59-64;
John 18:33-19:11

1. What could we regard as the seven energies of the Spirit?

2. How was Jesus a faithful witness?

Heavenly Father, thank You for the reminder that no matter how things appear, Your Son is in charge of the march of the moments. Help me never to forget this. In Christ's name. Amen.

Loved! Loosed! Lifted!

FOR READING & MEDITATION – REVELATION 1:5-8

'To him who loves us and has freed us from our sins by his blood ...
to be a kingdom and priests ...' (vv.5-6)

Consideration of Jesus' preeminence and glory inevitably leads John to heartfelt praise and adoration of his Lord. Is it any wonder that after contemplating the Saviour's titles he breaks into this awe-inspiring doxology?

He *loves us*, says John. That is how it all started. We could not resist the overtures of One who showed us such amazing affection. But more than that: He has 'freed us [or loosed us] from our sins'. The Authorised Version reads, 'Unto him that loved us, and *washed* us from our sins.' Both translations are admissible. We are washed first and then loosed, or freed. D.L. Moody once powerfully remarked that Jesus did not wash us and then love us; He loved us and then washed us. The point he was making was this: anyone could have loved us after we had been washed; only Jesus could have loved us before we were washed. Nor is that all. He has *lifted* us, continues John, and made us kings and priests to serve God. The mitre as well as the crown adorns our brow. As kings, God means us to reign over sin and self, and as priests, to represent the world before God and bind it by the chains of believing prayer to His feet! Loved! Loosed! Lifted! What a thought to prime the pump of praise in our hearts.

FURTHER STUDY

Ezek. 16:3-14;
Mark 5:1-20

1. How did the Lord respond to the despised child?

2. How was the man loved, loosed and lifted?

But there is still more. This glorious One is going to return some day, and those who pierced Him will lament that they turned away. His own people, however, knowing He is the Alpha and Omega – the beginning and the end – will rejoice at His coming. A little girl in Sunday school, when asked why Jesus was described as the Alpha and Omega, said, 'Because He is the Alphabet out of which God puts together all His promises.' He is.

O Father, I am so grateful to You for loving me, loosing me and lifting me. Thank You too for putting a mitre as well as a crown on my head. All praise and honour be to Your glorious name. Amen.

CWR Ministry Events

PLEASE PRAY FOR THE TEAM

ATE	EVENT	PLACE	PRESENTER(S)
May	Small Group Leaders' Evening	Waverley Abbey House	Andy Peck
9 May	Bible Discovery: 'The Pebble Who Became a Rock'	Pilgrim Hall	Philip Greenslade
May	Understanding Yourself, Understanding Others	WAH	Lynn & Andrew Penson
May	Insight into Dementia	WAH	Rosemary Hurtley
-21 May	Certificate in Counselling Supervision	WAH	Heather Churchill
May Jun	The Big Story	WAH	Philip Greenslade
un	Insight into Addictions	WAH	Andre Radmall
Jun	Women's Summer Day	WAH	Lynn Penson
6 Jun	Church in Transition	WAH	Andy Peck
-14 Jun	Introduction to Biblical Care and Counselling	PH	Angie Coombes & team
Jun	Summer Evening for Homegroups	PH	Elizabeth Hodkinson
Jun	Summer Evening for Homegroups	WAH	Andy Peck
-21 Jun	Woman to Woman	PH	Lynn Penson & team
Jun	Counselling Enquirers' Event	WAH	Counselling Team
-23 Jun	Bible Discovery Weekend	WAH	Philip Greenslade
Jun	How to Lead a Bible Study	WAH	Andy Peck
Jun	Summer Evening for Homegroups	PH	Elizabeth Hodkinson
Jun	Summer Evening for Homegroups	WAH	Andy Peck

Please also pray for students and tutors on our ongoing **BA in Counselling** programme at Waverley and Pilgrim Hall and our **Certificate and Diploma of Christian Counselling** and **MA in Integrative Psychotherapy** held at London School of Theology.

For further details and a full list of CWR's courses, phone **+44 (0)1252 784719** or visit the CWR website at **www.cwr.org.uk** Pilgrim Hall: **www.pilgrimhall.com**

A secret stair

FOR READING & MEDITATION - REVELATION 1:9-11

'On the Lord's Day I was in the Spirit, and I heard behind me
a loud voice like a trumpet ...' (v.10)

John's account of the revelation he received was written
from the island of Patmos to which he had been
banished because of the 'word of God and the testimony of
Jesus'. We are not told exactly why he was exiled, but the
Roman Empire came down hard on Christian activists at
this time, and John's great influence in the Church might
well have seemed a threat to the authorities.

Picture him there on that lonely island. He was probably
then an old man, and his banishment almost certainly
involved hard labour. He tells us that he is a 'brother and

**FURTHER
STUDY**

Gen. 28:10-17;
Acts 16:22-34

1. What was
Jacob not
aware of?

2. What was
Paul and Silas's
stairway to
heaven?

companion in the suffering and kingdom' (v.9),
but his exile must have seemed more like the
sharing of Christ's suffering than the sharing of
His kingdom. Yet although Rome could shut John
off from contact with fellow Christians, it was
powerless to sever his contact with the throne
of God. Though he was *on* Patmos, he was *in* the
Spirit – his heart and mind were caught up in the
contemplation of God. And he was to be given a
vision of the King and His kingdom that would
transform not only his own life, but the lives of
countless others who, down the centuries, have
studied his words. It was the Lord's Day when he
received his revelation, we read – the day of resurrection
and the Christian's bright and exciting 'first day'.

Think for a moment about these contrasting phrases: 'I …
was on the island of Patmos … On the Lord's Day I was in the
Spirit.' 'On the island' he was in exile, but 'in the Spirit' he
touched the magnificence and brilliance of another world.
Nothing can stop God getting through to us, no matter what
the circumstances. The Almighty is always able to find or,
if necessary, construct a secret stair to our soul.

**O Father, how reassured I am to know that nothing can ever stop
Your Word being transmitted to my heart. I am so grateful that
no matter how difficult the circumstances, heaven's mail always
gets through. Amen.**

The vision

FOR READING & MEDITATION - REVELATION 1:12-16

'... and among the lampstands was someone "like a son of man",
dressed in a robe reaching down to his feet ...' (v.13)

A voice like a trumpet commands the apostle to write
what he sees on a scroll and send it to the seven
churches in Asia. When John hears the voice he says, 'I
turned round to *see* the voice that was speaking to me'
(v.12, my emphasis). How can you *see* a voice? John may
here be pointing to the greatness of the One to whom he
turned – Jesus is *the* Voice, the Living Word.

When John turns he sees Christ standing amid seven
golden lampstands – the symbols of the seven churches.
The Saviour is wearing a robe that reaches down to His
feet, has a golden sash around His chest, His head
and hair are white as snow, His eyes like a blazing
fire, His feet as bronze, His voice is like the sound
of rushing waters, His face is as the sun, in His
right hand He holds seven stars, and from His
mouth comes a sharp double-edged sword. What
an astonishing sight it must have been. But what
does the vision suggest?

Clothing symbolises role, and here Jesus is
represented as a priest (Exod. 29:5), the One
through whom we have access to God. His head,
eyes and face speak of His character. No one is more
pure in character than Jesus. His feet of bronze indicate His
ability to subdue His enemies underfoot. His voice, like His
appearance, commands attention. The seven stars represent
the angels (or leaders) of the seven churches, and the sword
is symbolic of the sharpness and penetrating power of His
Word. This is no longer the Socratic Jesus reasoning with
Pharisees and Sadducees, no longer a crucified Christ
nailed to a cross. No greater description of Jesus is to be
found anywhere in the Word of God. This is the picture of
Jesus I always hold before me when I pray.

FURTHER STUDY

Exod. 28:29;
29:5-9;
Luke 9:28-32

1. How was
Aaron a type
of Christ?

2. What did the
disciples see?

**Lord Jesus Christ, Son of Man and Son of God, may this vision
of Your glory so fill my heart that it will transform every part
of me, especially my prayer life. In Your precious name I ask it.
Amen.**

'What you have seen ... write'

FOR READING & MEDITATION – REVELATION 1:17-20

'I am the Living One; I was dead, and behold I am alive for ever and ever!' (v.18)

It is not surprising that the vision of the glorified Christ causes John to fall into a dead faint! The hand which held the seven stars is placed upon him, and the voice like the sound of rushing waters says, 'Do not be afraid.' These same words, you remember, transformed Simon Peter's terror to trust on the storm-tossed lake (Matt. 14:27), and brought peace and reassurance to Mary Magdalene after she had found Jesus' tomb empty (Matt. 28:10). John soon revives, and his fear abates as he realises he is in the presence of his Creator – the First and the Last – who tells him, 'I was dead, and behold I am alive for ever and ever! And I hold the keys of death and Hades.'

FURTHER STUDY

Exod. 17:8-14;
Luke 1:1-14

1. Why was Moses to write?

2. Why did Luke write?

Then John is instructed, 'Write … what you have seen' (v.19). If you will permit a personal reflection here, these were the words God used in 1965 to start me on a writing career. I came to the Scriptures looking for a directive to confirm the desire growing within me to begin writing daily Bible notes, and this was the message that sealed it. The Spirit quickened those words to my heart. Ever since that time I have been trying to write what I have seen.

The vision sets John on the task of making known the mystery of the seven stars and the seven golden lampstands – the seven stars being the angels (or leaders) and the seven lampstands the seven churches. How amazing it must have been for John to realise that there was a correlation and connection between what happened to the seven communities of faith he knew so well and the movements of heaven. It will help us as we face today, tomorrow and the days beyond to remember that nothing can ever happen on earth that is not anticipated in eternity.

Father, I have started with this vision of Christ; help me never to let it go. May He fill my mind and dominate my life in the same way that He dominates this book. For His name's sake. Amen.

The three Rs

FOR READING & MEDITATION - REVELATION 2:1-7

'Yet I hold this against you: You have forsaken your first love.' (v.4)

We turn now to the next great theme – the Church. 'The gospel,' it has been said, 'is never for individuals but always for a community.' What is meant by that statement, I think, is that although salvation is highly personal, it is never merely individual. We are called to live in relationship with others. The revelation of Jesus is not just for John, but for the seven churches in Asia. Why *seven* churches when we know there were at least ten? The seven churches stand for all churches.

The first church addressed is that in Ephesus. Jesus introduces Himself as the One 'who holds the seven stars in his right hand and walks among the seven golden lampstands' (v.1) as if to say: 'I am your Senior Pastor … the One who sees all and knows all.' The letter opens with a commendation, which is followed by a condemnation, and then concludes with a command. First the commendation: 'I know your deeds' (v.2). The believers in Ephesus were faithful, industrious and toiling to the point of exhaustion. But although Jesus commends them for this, they are condemned because they have left their first love. What good is duty without devotion? Hearts that had once been on fire with love for the Lord had now chilled.

Jesus then provides the way and outlines the process for recapturing that lost love: remember, repent and return. The Ephesians were to remember the way things had been, what had happened to chill their affection, to repent and return to a close relationship with the Saviour. If they did not, they were warned, their lampstand would be removed. It is unspeakably sad when a church has no love in it, for where there is no love there can be no light.

FURTHER STUDY

John 15:13;
1 Pet. 1:3-9;
1 John 4:7-21

1. Why do we love the Lord?

2. How do we know we love the Lord?

O God, forgive us that our light shines so dimly in the world because we love so weakly. Help us to remember how things once were, to repent of our lost love and to return to an intimate relationship with You. In Jesus' name. Amen.

Fearful but faithful

FOR READING & MEDITATION - REVELATION 2:8-11
'Do not be afraid of what you are about to suffer ...
Be faithful, even to the point of death ...' (v.10)

The second letter is addressed to the church in Smyrna. If love was the key word for the Ephesians, the key word for the believers in Smyrna was *suffering*. At the time Revelation was written (probably about AD 95), Smyrna was the pride of Asia. It is, in fact, the only one of the seven cities named still thriving, and is known today as Izmir.

Great suffering was to fall upon the church at Smyrna, and Jesus begins by reminding them that He is 'the First and the Last, who died and came to life again' (v.8). This is always the manner in which Jesus seeks to comfort His people in times of distress; He reminds us that He knows all, and of the truth that His overcoming life is ours for the taking. Jesus was well aware of their poverty (probably the result of the refusal of Smyrna's citizens to do business with Christians), and also the slander they received from the Jewish community. But He encourages them to continue being faithful, promising them an eternal reward.

FURTHER STUDY

2 Cor. 4:7-5:8

1. How did Paul view suffering?

2. How did Paul view death?

In the message to the Ephesians the overcomer's reward was to eat from the tree of life. Here the figure is changed. It is now a crown of life – a term used to describe the wreath or trophy awarded to the victor at the games. The suffering Christians of Smyrna needed to know that a trophy of victory awaited them in eternity. Sadly, more Christians were martyred for their faith in the twentieth century than in the previous nineteen centuries combined, and a huge number face martyrdom even today. The prospect of being forced to give up one's life for the cause of Christ is not pleasant, but for a Christian death is not the end; it is the prelude to a new and joyously endless life shared with Jesus Himself.

O Father, wherever Your children are being persecuted or are under threat of death, give them a special supply of Your grace, I pray. Deliver them from fear and help them stand firm for You no matter what. In Christ's name I ask this. Amen.

FOR READING & MEDITATION - REVELATION 2:12-17

'Repent therefore! Otherwise, I will soon come to you and will fight against them with the sword of my mouth.' (v.16)

We reflect now on the words of Jesus to the church in Pergamum. The city of Pergamum lay about 60 miles north of Smyrna, and at the time these letters were addressed to the churches it was known to be a strong centre of emperor-worship and idolatry, 'where Satan has his throne' (v.13). Jesus' key word to this church was *truth*. In Pergamum there was conflict between truth and error.

To this church Jesus reveals Himself as the One who has 'the sharp, double-edged sword' (v.12), demonstrating that He will overcome false doctrine. St Augustine said that Christ's double-edged sword consists of the Old and New Testaments, and he added, 'We need both if we are to overcome error.' Though false doctrines were circulating in the church in Pergamum, many still held fast to the truth, one member having been martyred for his refusal to renounce his belief (v.13).

The error accepted by some at Pergamum was similar to that of Balaam's day. To understand the reference in verse 14 we need to compare Numbers 31:16 with Numbers chapter 25. Balaam suggested to Balak, king of Moab, that young Moabite women should seduce the men of Israel and persuade them to worship idols, knowing that such behaviour would bring upon them the wrath of God. What Balaam was to ancient Israel, the Nicolaitans were to the church in Pergamum. Jesus' face is always set against a church community where error is propagated and sin is tolerated. But He again closes with a promise to those who overcome: 'hidden manna' and 'a white stone with a new name on it' – sustenance in an alien environment and a new title given by Jesus, signifying our intimate relationship with Him.

FURTHER STUDY

Num. 25:1-13; 31:16;
Gal. 5:16-25

1. How did the Israelites lose a fight without fighting?

2. With which conflict are we involved?

Lord Jesus Christ, who can win a fight against You? May we Your people set our faces against every kind of sin so that we might flourish in relationship with You. For Your own dear name's sake. Amen.

A holy people

FOR READING & MEDITATION - REVELATION 2:18-29

'Nevertheless, I have this against you: You tolerate that woman Jezebel, who calls herself a prophetess.' (v.20)

The next message from Jesus is to the church in Thyatira. This church appeared to be flourishing spiritually, with good works, love, service, faith and perseverance blossoming as in a beautiful garden. Jesus introduces Himself to this church as 'the Son of God, whose eyes are like blazing fire and whose feet are like burnished bronze' (v.18). There was good reason for the church to see Jesus in this role as, despite its pleasing appearance, a pernicious sin was destroying them. They needed, therefore, to see Christ as the One whose eyes burned with the fire of righteous indignation against sin, and whose feet were capable of trampling them to powder.

FURTHER STUDY

Titus 2:11-15;
James 5:19-20

1. What does God's grace do?

2. How should we respond to those who wander from truth?

The operative word to the church at Ephesus was love, to the church at Smyrna it was suffering, to the church at Pergamum it was truth, and to the church in Thyatira it was *holiness*. Although quite clearly the church manifested a number of graces, holiness was not one of them. A woman in the church was acting like Jezebel, the wife of Ahab (see 1 Kings 16:31), and encouraging Christians to practise immorality and eat food sacrificed to idols.

Again we see the Jesus who is against any church where immorality is practised. When there is repentance, however, and the church shines as a light in a dark world, then Christ will be seen as the morning star who, as one commentator puts it, 'is the assurance of the coming dawn when lamplight will be swallowed up in the light of eternal day'. Jesus' encouragement to the church in Thyatira, and to us today, is to 'hold on' until He comes. And those who do are promised the gift of Jesus Himself, who will enable them to be the shining light He made them to be.

O God my Father, how we need this emphasis on holiness in an age when almost anything goes - even in Your Church. Give us a new vision of holiness and help us all become a more holy people. In Jesus' name. Amen.

The living water, with love ...

... from you, to Christians without means, both at home and overseas, who - like you - thirst for a life truly led according to God's will. A gift to the guiding ministry of CWR can secure the faith of many.

'For the Lamb at the centre of the throne will be their shepherd; he will lead them to springs of living water. And God will wipe away every tear from their eyes.' Revelation 7:17

Please help CWR to provide resources to satisfy the thirst of many.

Please fill in the 'Gift to CWR' section on the order form at the back of this publication, completing the Gift Aid declaration if appropriate.

Wake up!

FOR READING & MEDITATION - REVELATION 3:1-6

'But if you do not wake up, I will come like a thief, and you will not know at what time I will come to you.' (v.3)

We come now to the letter to the church in Sardis. Christ introduces Himself as the One 'who holds the seven spirits of God and the seven stars' (v.1). As we have already noted, the phrase 'the seven spirits of God' refers to the manifold energies of the one Holy Spirit ministering to each of the seven churches at the same time. But why does Jesus begin by laying emphasis on the ministry of the Spirit? Because, I believe, this was their greatest need. Not so much love, suffering, truth or holiness, but *life*.

Clearly the church at Sardis had gained a reputation for being a progressive and lively centre of witness, but the outward appearance was deceptive. Jesus saw them as being nothing more than a morgue with a steeple. All those around would have regarded the church at Sardis as a flourishing, active, successful church – all except Jesus Himself. 'Wake up!' is His command to them. 'Strengthen what remains and is about to die' (v.2). The church at Sardis was desperately in need of revival. In all the other churches Jesus finds something to commend, but for this one there is no word of commendation, only condemnation. A few were still thriving spiritually, and to them Jesus promises His presence in a powerful way (v.4). However, in the main the church was dead, a spiritual graveyard. How sad.

FURTHER STUDY

Eph. 5:8-20;
1 Thess. 5:1-11

1. What are Paul's warnings?

2. What are Paul's instructions?

Unfortunately, this is true of some of today's churches which have a name for being alive but do not allow the Holy Spirit to work in their midst; they have ceremony but no life, pageantry but no Pentecost. These churches need to 'wake up'. If the Holy Spirit is not welcomed and allowed to have His way in a church, then it no longer functions as a church; sadly, it is merely a club.

Gracious and loving Father, help us open our hearts to the whole Trinity - Father, Son and Holy Spirit. Let there be no 'missing member' in the Church of the twenty-first century. In Jesus' name I pray. Amen.

A global perspective

FOR READING & MEDITATION - REVELATION 3:7-13

'See, I have placed before you an open door that no-one
can shut.' (v.8)

The next church we consider is the church in Philadelphia. Whereas the church in Sardis received almost unmitigated condemnation, the church in Philadelphia receives almost unqualified commendation. Jesus approaches this church by informing them He is 'holy and true, who holds the key of David' (v.7). The image of a key is used because He is to open for them a door of opportunity (v.8). The word *opportunity* probably best summarises Jesus' message to the church in Philadelphia.

What was this open door? Almost certainly an opportunity not just to stand firm but to take the good news to the known world. Philadelphia was strategically placed, standing as it did at the junction of the routes to the regions of Mysia, Lydia, and Phrygia. William M. Ramsay, in his *Letters to the Seven Churches*, likens those in the church at Philadelphia to 'archers, bow bent, and ready to thrust arrows deep into the heart of the interior'. Christians in Philadelphia were not a strong congregation (v.8), and faced a great deal of outside opposition. But through the door opened to them they would go out and bring others in. A church of little strength was to become mighty in winning souls to Christ and would be established as an immovable pillar in the temple of the new Jerusalem, the city of God (v.12). While the contemporary Church needs to hear the message of love, suffering, truth, holiness and life, it needs also to see that it has a greater opportunity to share the good news than at any other time in history. Radio, television, the internet – all are open doors. We must go through those doors with a global perspective and say with John Wesley, 'All the world is my parish.'

FURTHER STUDY

Matt. 28:16-20;
Acts 1:6-8;
Col. 4:2-6

1. How are you fulfilling the Great Commission?

2. What are we to pray for?

O Father, forgive us that in an age when there is a communication explosion we are so slow to use our opportunities to present the gospel. Forgive us, restore us and quicken us, we pray. In Jesus' name. Amen.

You make me sick!

FOR READING & MEDITATION - REVELATION 3:14-22

'So, because you are lukewarm - neither hot nor cold
- I am about to spit you out of my mouth.' (v.16)

Jesus' seventh and final letter is addressed to the church in Laodicea. To this church Christ presents Himself as 'the Amen, the faithful and true witness, the ruler of God's creation' (v.14). The church needed to see Him as the One who remains constant and reliable in the midst of flux and change. There can be no doubt that a change had taken place in the Laodicean church – a change for the worse. They had become spiritually lukewarm. To drink lukewarm water is an unpleasant experience, and Jesus uses this analogy in His comment on the church: 'I wish you were either one or the other!' (v.15). What a statement – that Jesus prefers cold Christianity to the lukewarm variety!

FURTHER STUDY

John 2:12-17;
James 1:19-27

1. What is the example of Jesus?

2. How might we be deceived?

Laodicea was a wealthy textile town famous for its manufacture of black woollen clothing, lukewarm supply of water channelled from hot springs, and special eye ointment. Yet though the believers considered themselves rich, Christ tells them they are 'wretched, pitiful, poor, blind and naked' (v.17). And yet despite all this, Jesus still loves His people and counsels them to come to Him in earnest repentance. Is there any picture more compelling than Christ standing at the door of His own Church seeking readmittance (v.20)?

You may have noticed that at the end of each of His messages to the churches Jesus exhorts them to hear what the Spirit is saying. This need to pay attention is emphasised because we are such poor listeners. We hear the words but we don't get the point. To hear what the Spirit says and not apply it to ourselves is one of the greatest tragedies. Let's make sure it doesn't happen.

O Father, save me from hearing yet still failing to hear. Help me understand the point of everything You say to me and apply it to my soul. I ask this in the Saviour's precious name. Amen.

Our God reigns

FOR READING & MEDITATION - REVELATION 4:1-3

'Come up here, and I will show you what must take place after this.'

(v.1)

We come now to the next great theme of Revelation – *worship*. It is worth noting that in the first three chapters of Revelation Jesus is not seen except in the company of His Church. Some would prefer to move from chapter 1, where we catch sight of the magnificent Christ, to chapter 4, where we find the most marvellous worship, without having to negotiate the business of the flawed Church. But, as Eugene Peterson says, 'Christ is not *apart* from the gathered, listening, praying, believing, worshipping people to whom He is Lord and Saviour. It is just not possible to have Christ apart from His Church.'

In the verses before us today we read that John observes a door standing open in heaven, and once again he hears the voice like a trumpet calling him to come. As he enters through the door the first thing he sees is a rainbow-encircled throne 'with someone sitting on it' (v.2). Do you recall how a vision of the heavenly throne sustained the Old Testament prophets Isaiah (Isa. 6:1), Ezekiel (Ezek. 1:26; 10:1), and Daniel (Dan. 7:9)? Why a throne – God's throne? In Bible times a monarch reigned from his throne. It was the symbol of authority. By giving a vision of His throne, God seeks to reassure His people that no matter what happens on earth, the final seat of authority is in heaven.

The early Russian Communists used to say, 'We will depose the kings from their thrones on earth and then we will depose God from His throne in the sky.' Not so, says the writer to the Hebrews: 'Your throne, O God, will last for ever and ever' (Heb. 1:8). Other thrones may be toppled, but not God's throne. Our God reigns – eternally.

FURTHER STUDY

Psa. 2:1-12; 100:1-5

1. What causes God to laugh?

2. How do we enter God's presence?

O God, how reassuring it is in an age when so many thrones have been toppled to know that Your throne will never be overturned. It is from everlasting to everlasting. Thank You, my Father. Amen.

Nothing more wonderful

FOR READING & MEDITATION - REVELATION 4:3-5

'And the one who sat there had the appearance of jasper and carnelian.' (v.3)

Yesterday we said that in Old Testament times God sought to encourage His discouraged people with a vision of His throne. It was His way of showing them that no matter what happens on earth, the final authority rests in heaven. In John's vision not only the throne captivated his attention, but also the One who sat upon it. Stretching words to their limit, he compares the appearance of the throne's occupant to that of 'jasper and carnelian'.

The *NIV Commentary* says, 'Since God dwells in unapproachable light and is One whom no one has seen or can see, He is described in terms of the reflected brilliance of precious stones.' Light, scientists inform us, is full of colour, all colours, but our eyes are unable to fully detect them. One commentator explains it like this: 'A "precious" stone, selecting certain colours out of the air and intensifying them, shows us the deep colour that is in light all the time.' It was from this colour-laden throne, we must remember, that the command 'Let there be light' first went forth (Gen. 1:3).

Here on earth light is often filtered through polluted air, and rarely do we see colours as they really are. Then we pick up a precious stone and glimpse a brilliant blue or a glorious green and stand in awe once again. Something similar happens to us as we draw near to God's throne to worship; the light from this rainbow-encircled throne bathes our souls so that holiness, grace, truth and love shine with their true colours. It is in the act of worship that the qualities God has so graciously given show up most clearly, most sharply. Only in His light can we see – really see. I tell you, nothing illuminates and enriches the soul more than worship.

FURTHER STUDY

James 1:16-18;
Rev. 21:9-27

1. How does James describe God?

2. Why is there no natural or artificial light in heaven?

O Father, I can only feebly comprehend the impact that the worship of You has upon my soul. Right now I draw near to worship You. Please draw near to me. In Jesus' name. Amen.

FOR READING & MEDITATION – REVELATION 4:5-8

'From the throne came flashes of lightning, rumblings and peals of thunder.' (v.5)

Before we turn our gaze from the throne to that which surrounds it, permit me to quote Eugene Peterson's thoughts on the significance of God's eternal throne. 'The throne of God – the fact of the throne, and the fact of God enthroned,' he says, 'is the supreme revelation of the Bible. All rejection is rejection of divine government, all peace comes from an acceptance of God's right rule in His universe.'

John observes before the throne 'what looked like a sea of glass, clear as crystal' (v.6). In order for worshippers to get close to the throne it is necessary to pass through the 'crystal sea'. It is suggestive of the fact that worshippers are to be cleansed and sanctified as they draw near. There are those who think worship involves simply going out into the country and thinking about God. But true worship involves first a cleansing, a purifying. 'Without holiness no-one will see [or worship] the Lord' (Heb. 12:14).

In addition to the representative people around the throne mentioned in verse 4 (probably the 12 patriarchs and 12 apostles), John sees representative animals (v.6). The first was like a lion, the second like an ox, the third had a face like that of a human being, and the fourth was like a flying eagle. These four creatures represent aspects of creation: the lion, nobility; the ox, strength; the human, wisdom; the eagle, swiftness. Hebrew patriarchs, Christian apostles, human beings, animals, birds – all surround the throne as a testimony to the fact that they are what they are because God is who He is. God desires that all creation worship Him, not because He is egotistic, but because, as C.S. Lewis finely put it, 'Worship is the right response to such a creator as this.'*

FURTHER STUDY

Psa. 148:1-14; 150:1-6

1. Who should worship the Lord?

2. What should worship the Lord?

Father, as I reflect on the wonder of Your creation, I want to echo the words of Francis of Assisi: 'All creatures of our God and King, lift up your voice and with us sing.' As I contemplate Your glory my heart truly *sings*. Amen.

Dazzling splendour

FOR READING & MEDITATION - REVELATION 4:9-11

'You are worthy, our Lord and God, to receive glory and honour and power ...' (v.11)

The scene before us now is one of the most moving in the whole of Scripture. As the living creatures are giving glory, the 24 elders fall down before the throne and worship Him who lives for ever and ever. The elders remove their crowns and place them before Him who sits on the throne, acknowledging that God alone is worthy of ultimate praise and worship. Aloud they cry, 'You are worthy, our Lord and God, to receive glory and honour and power, for you created all things, and by your will they were created and have their being.'

FURTHER STUDY

1 Chron. 29:10-20; Rom. 12:1-2

1. What did David acknowledge?

2. How can we worship?

New Christians often ask: Why does God want us to worship Him? Is it because He can't function without the compliments of His creation? Permit me to quote C.S. Lewis again. 'Praise,' he said, 'is inner health made audible.' In other words, we become better for having worshipped, for in the act of worship our personalities are made healthy. 'Going through the door of worship,' he claimed, 'we complete ourselves; we become all that we were meant to be.'* Edmund P. Clowney puts it like this: 'God is the centre of all things. We worship so that we live in response to and from this centre, the living God. Failure to worship consigns us to a life of spasms and jerks, at the mercy of every advertisement, every seduction. If there is no centre there is no circumference. People who do not worship are swept into a vast restlessness ... with no steady direction and no sustaining purpose.'

There is really only one way to go in a universe that was called into being by the Word of the Creator, and that is the way of worship. If we do not know how to worship we do not know how to live – period.

O Father, I accept that unless I know how to worship I remain a stunted soul - incomplete. Teach me to worship You in spirit and in truth, I pray. For if I do not worship I do not truly live. Help me, my Father. In Jesus' name. Amen.

Why unanswered prayer?

FOR READING & MEDITATION - REVELATION 5:1-8

'Then I saw a Lamb, looking as if it had been slain, standing in the centre of the throne ...' (v.6)

In the midst of the glory of the rainbow-encircled throne, John becomes aware that in the right hand of Him who sits upon it is an unopened scroll, sealed with seven seals. A mighty angel shouts, 'Who is worthy to break the seals and open the scroll?' (v.2). When no one comes forward John finds himself overcome with emotion. 'I wept and wept,' he says (v.4).

Commentators disagree as to the meaning of the scroll. Some believe that it represents Scripture, the written Word, whose truth can be understood only as it is revealed by the living Word. Others maintain it is the title deeds to the earth itself. It is more important, though, to watch what happens after Jesus opens it. One of the elders says to John, 'See, the Lion of the tribe of Judah ...' (v.5). John lifts his eyes, expecting to see a lion, but instead he sees a Lamb 'looking as if it had been slain'.

What are we to make of this? Jesus, God's Lamb, possesses all that is necessary for our redemption. Though He has the gentleness of a lamb, He has also the strength of a lion. The moment the Lamb takes the scroll heaven breaks into jubilation, and the living creatures and the 24 elders fall down before Him. Each one has a harp and also a golden bowl full of incense representing the prayers (presumably the unanswered prayers) of the saints. One commentator suggests that the biggest problem people cry out to God about in their prayers is this: 'Why, Lord, do You permit evil to continue?' Here on earth we will never fully understand, but because of John's vision, we have the hope that one day evil will be overturned completely.

FURTHER STUDY

Isa. 53:1-12; John 1:29-34

1. Why are people depicted as sheep?

2. Why is Jesus depicted as a lamb?

O Father, I recognise that this cry arises from time to time in my own heart too. Why do You allow evil to have such seemingly unhindered sway? I am thankful that though I may not fully understand, You give me grace to fully stand. Amen.

New MA Counselling Programme

On Tuesday 24 July 2012, CWR was proud to celebrate the achievement of the first graduates from our BA (Hons) Counselling programme and Diploma of Higher Education, as they received their degrees from the University of Roehampton. Following a thanksgiving and commissioning service at Waverley Abbey House, a total of 25 students attended the graduation ceremony held at Guildford Cathedral.

Increasingly known for our Waverley Model, our ministry continues to expand with an exciting new opportunity to develop plans for an MA in Christian Counselling. This will be available to graduates from a range of professional backgrounds who have already acquired counselling skills and now wish to train at postgraduate level.

The course will enable students to deepen their knowledge through the study of a range of theoretical models and the evaluation of research methods and practice. Students will also extend their personal counselling skills and competence, developing greater self-awareness through reflective practice.

Learning, which will meet academic standards, will take place in a supportive, lively context which encourages reflective thinking. The distinctive feature of this course is the fact that it is underpinned by a Christian worldview starting from the premise that human beings are created in the image of God, designed for a relationship with Him and each other. Graduates will, however, be trained to work ethically and professionally in a variety of situations with clients of all faiths or none.

The MA will be a three-year, part-time, programme, leading to a Post-Graduate Certificate after one year, a Post-Graduate Diploma after two years, and a Masters degree after three years.

Teaching sessions will be concentrated in the first two years of the programme and will take place over six long weekends (from Thursday evening to Sunday lunchtime) each year. A dissertation will be written in the third year. In addition, students will arrange client placements in years 1 and 2, achieving at least 75 client hours per year.

Initially, the course will be offered in the UK at Pilgrim Hall, East Sussex. Subject to approval by the University of Roehampton, our hope is that it will then subsequently also be offered in Singapore.

To find out more, please book to join us on a Counselling Open Morning on 21 June 2013 between 10am and 1pm at Waverley Abbey House, Surrey. Alternatively, to register your interest and be kept in touch with further developments, please contact the Assistant Registrar, Donna Maddox at **dmaddox@cwr.org.uk** or on **01252 784731**.

A song par excellence

FOR READING & MEDITATION - REVELATION 5:9-10

'And they sang a new song: "You are worthy to take the scroll and to open its seals, because you were slain ..."' (v.9)

As you may be aware, singing and songs are constantly threaded throughout Scripture. At creation we read that the angelic host shouted and sang for joy (Job 38:7). Moses sang (Exod. 15:1). Miriam sang (Exod. 15:21). Deborah sang (Judg. 5:1). David sang (2 Sam. 22:1). Mary sang (Luke 1:46). Jesus and His disciples sang (Matt. 26:30). Paul and Silas sang (Acts 16:25). It seems that singing just cannot be repressed in the people of God. But nowhere in the Bible do we find a song like this. It is a song not merely about the goodness of God, but a specific song of redemption. And it is described as a *new* song. In the Old Testament a new song celebrated a new act of divine deliverance or intervention, and that is its purpose here. Heaven now has a song *par excellence* – a song about the ransom paid for sinners by the Son of God Himself.

FURTHER STUDY

Psa. 98:1-9;
1 Pet. 1:18-23

1. What was the cause of the psalmist's worship?

2. What is unique about Christ's sacrifice?

Look back for a moment to the words in Revelation 5:6 – 'a Lamb, looking as if it had been slain' – we find there the assurance that the marks of Jesus' suffering will be seen in heaven for all eternity. As the old hymn puts it: 'Those wounds, yet visible above [are] in beauty glorified.' Every element of worship is wonderful, but the highest note surely must be the fact that we have been made clean, redeemed and set free by His sacrifice. In this angels cannot join us for they have not been redeemed.

Notice in verse 10 the phrase 'a *kingdom* and priests' (italics mine). Three times this phrase occurs in Revelation. And for this reason. In Christ Jesus we are lifted (as we saw earlier) not only to the dignity of priesthood but also to the splendour of royalty. We have a crown on our head as well as a censer in our hand.

Gracious and loving heavenly Father, how can I ever sufficiently thank You for the honour You have bestowed upon me? May I show myself worthy of such honour. For Your own dear name's sake. Amen.

'Oh, Yes!'

FOR READING & MEDITATION – REVELATION 5:11-14

'The four living creatures said, "Amen", and the elders fell down and worshipped.' (v.14)

Five songs are sung in the act of worship depicted for us in Revelation 4 and 5. The first song is adoration of the being of God: 'Holy, holy, holy is the Lord God Almighty, who was, and is, and is to come' (4:8). The second is a song about God's creative power (4:11). The third song – the *new* song – is to Christ, the Lamb of God (5:9-10). The fourth and fifth are the ones occupying our attention now.

The fourth song (5:12) begins like the third, uses the ascription of the second, but is sung by 'many angels' whose number cannot be counted. They focus their praise on the Lamb but, as we indicated yesterday, their praise can only be objective, never subjective. In the words of the hymn by Johnson Oatman Jr: 'Angels never knew the joy that my salvation brings.' The fifth song (5:13) joins together the blessings of creation and redemption and is sung by the whole of creation. Imagine hearing, one day, every voice in creation being lifted in adoration of God and the Lamb!

FURTHER STUDY

Luke 1:46-79

1. How did Mary say 'Oh, Yes'?

2. How did Zechariah say 'Oh, Yes'?

The last word that we hear as we contemplate this wondrous worship is 'Amen'. I love the way Eugene Peterson in *The Message* translates the word 'Amen': 'Oh Yes!' He calls it 'the last word in worship', and goes on to say: 'Amen means "Yes"'. It is the worshipping affirmation to the God who affirms us. When we come to God in worship we are immersed in God's Yes, a yes that silences all our no's and calls forth an answering yes in us. We respond to His yes by saying, 'Yes.' How wonderful it is when a congregation responds to someone's prayers with a vigorous 'Amen'. Sadly, the practice seems to be dying out in many modern-day churches, but I'm glad to know it is still practised in heaven.

Father, as I see the whole universe engaged in worshipping You and listen to their songs of praise, my heart wants to join in. I do so now – with my whole heart. I worship You, dear Father. Oh, Yes!

Leading the charge

FOR READING & MEDITATION - REVELATION 6:1-2

'Its rider held a bow, and he was given a crown, and he rode out as a conqueror bent on conquest.' (v.2)

We consider now another great theme of Revelation – how Jesus finally overcomes and how we, as His servants, can also overcome. If the pre-eminent Christ who towers over everything in the opening chapter of Revelation is so powerful, we may wonder, then why is it that evil still continues to wreak havoc? And will evil eventually be vanquished? This is the issue which is brought into focus in chapters 6 and 7.

It is largely from here onwards that interpretations of Revelation differ. One group (preterists) see it applying only to the first century. Another group (historicists) take it as describing the long chain of events from John's day to the end of time. A third group (futurists) place events outlined in the book primarily in the end times. A fourth group (idealists) view it as containing symbolic pictures which trigger the imagination and enable us to feel more powerfully the impact that Jesus Christ makes on history. My purpose in these meditations, as I said in the introduction, is to focus on its *overall* message and apply it devotionally. Fortunately the overall message does not depend on adopting a particular view.

FURTHER STUDY

John 10:7-10;
Heb. 2:9-18;
1 John 3:18

1. Why did the devil come?

2. Why did Jesus come?

We begin chapter 6 with John's description of the first of the seven seals being opened by the Lamb. The voice of one of the living creatures cries, 'Come', whereupon John sees a white horse on which sits a rider with a bow in his hand who is given a crown. This rider, a warrior bent on conquest, is most likely a representative of Christ (see also 19:11) who is first in the battle against sin and evil. The word 'evil', it has often been pointed out, is the word 'live' spelt backwards. Sin has blotted the universe by taking life and turning it into evil. Jesus is leading the charge for restoration.

O Father, I am so grateful that You are not content to wage the battle against evil from Your throne. You sent Your Son into the thick of it. He is always the first on the field of battle. Help me not to be afraid of joining in. Amen.

Right use of the Spirit

FOR READING & MEDITATION - REVELATION 6:3-8

'When the Lamb opened the second seal, I heard the second living creature say, "Come!"' (v.3)

Yesterday we looked at the first of the famous 'Four Horses of the Apocalypse' – the white horse – and its rider, which, we said, may represent Christ, who is first on the field in the battle against evil. As the white horse recedes from John's vision he observes the opening of the second seal, and the appearance of a bright red horse and its rider. The fact that the rider was given power to take away peace, and was given a large sword, clearly indicates that he was involved in waging war. This kind of war is evil, no matter how it may be rationalised. 'Our Lord,' says one commentator, 'does not sit on the red horse – ever.'

When the Lamb opens the third seal a black horse appears, whose rider holds in his hands a pair of scales. The context leads us to believe that this horse and horseman are symbolic of scarcity and famine. Famine, too, is a terrible evil. Who has not sat appalled at the sight of the victims of famine, who feature so frequently on our television screens? When the fourth seal is opened a pale horse appears whose rider is named Death. This horse and its rider are symbolic of sickness and epidemic disease.

FURTHER STUDY

Luke 8:41-56; 9:12-17

1. How did Jesus respond to sickness and death?

2. How did Jesus respond to hunger?

These three horsemen stand for three of the greatest evils in the world – war, famine and sickness which leads to death. What is being said here is that Jesus has set His face against them and will ultimately overcome them. Whatever form of evil you encounter today be assured of this: Jesus is there ahead of you riding into battle against its forces. Let us open ourselves afresh to the Holy Spirit so that in His strength and power we might move forward with confidence and in the hope of all that Jesus will accomplish for us.

My Father and my God, forgive us that we Your people are more ready to enjoy the thrill that Your power produces in us than we are to use it in the battle against evil. Forgive us and restore us. In Jesus' name we pray. Amen.

Hold on

FOR READING & MEDITATION – REVELATION 6:9-11

'How long, Sovereign Lord, holy and true, until you judge the inhabitants of the earth and avenge our blood?' (v.10)

Earlier we saw that John wept because there was no one to open the scroll (5:4). Then Jesus Christ, in the form of a Lamb, came forward and, one by one, as the seals are opened, the major incarnations of the evil that have filled this world are identified. However, as we said, because Jesus is first on the field of battle against evil and is 'bent on conquest' (6:2), we can rest assured that evil will ultimately be overcome – we have a future hope.

With the opening of the fifth seal another kind of evil is exposed – the evil of religious persecution. John sees under the altar the souls of those who had died because of their commitment to God's Word, and hears them crying out, 'How long?' This represents the sacrificial nature of the martyrs' death. It is probable that they are described as being 'under the altar' because that is where the blood of animals sacrificed on the altar was poured out (see Lev. 4:7).

FURTHER STUDY

Acts 7:54-60;
12:1-17

1. What did Stephen see when persecuted?

2. Contrast the experiences of James and Peter.

Why does God allow His people to be persecuted? We know that He is not powerless to deliver them. Why, then, are they allowed to suffer? Though we have some insights, such as that we are tested through suffering and that tribulation produces patience, we will have to wait until we get to heaven for the full answer. What we do know, however, is that Jesus is filled with compassion for those who suffer and, after giving the martyrs a white robe – a symbol of blessedness and purity – they are told to 'wait a little longer' (v.11). The mark of the faithful is that they hold on. And this is not just to a philosophy, but to a Person – they can cling to Jesus.

Father, I praise You that though You do not always remove trials You always provide sufficient grace for me to bear them and carry on. For this I am so grateful. Amen.

No peaceful co-existence

FOR READING & MEDITATION - REVELATION 6:12-17

'For the great day of their wrath has come, and who can stand?'
(v.17)

The opening of the sixth seal by the Lamb brings about a great cataclysm – the shaking of the cosmos. Everything in heaven and earth falls apart. The world is in chaos. No one can stand upright – no king, no prince, no general, no ordinary citizen. Many regard this as depicting the end of the world, but it can also be seen as a graphic picture of a natural catastrophe which causes those who are not standing firm in Jesus Christ to topple into despair. Follow the line of thought introduced by the opening of the seals with me once again: war, famine, death, religious persecution, and now, natural catastrophe.

The images in this passage are extremely vivid and strike the imagination with tremendous force. That is exactly what they are intended to do. We must, however, be careful about the symbolism here. These verses may well point to the natural disasters of our time as signs of Jesus' soon return. Yet, in the Old Testament, this sort of language was often employed as a way of speaking about 'earth-shattering events' of history, when people realise they are at the mercy of the God who rules the world. The graphic descriptions are designed to shock us, to make us recognise reality, to help us have no illusions about the depravity and evil that exist in the midst of God's fair creation. The book of Revelation brings everything out into the open; there is no glossing over matters, no sugar-coating of the bitter facts.

The chapter ends with the question: 'Who can stand?' The answer is clear – no one. Those who live by evil shall perish by evil. Evil has the smell of death upon it. It may prosper for a time but its end is certain.

FURTHER STUDY

Genesis 19:14-29;
2 Pet. 3:3-10

1. What happened to different members of Lot's community?

2. Why might God postpone judgment?

O Father, I see from these graphic depictions that You want to stir up a righteous anger in me against all forms of depravity. Help me not to be reconciled to evil but to resist it in every way I can. For Jesus' sake. Amen.

More than a match

FOR READING & MEDITATION - REVELATION 7:1-8

'After this I saw four angels standing at the four corners
of the earth ...' (v.1)

We noted yesterday that chapter 6 of Revelation ends with a question: 'Who can stand?' The answer, I believe, is clear: no one. That statement now needs to be qualified, for we see here angels at work. *They* can stand. *They* are not intimidated by evil. The issue seems so important that for a little while there is a delay in the opening of the seventh seal. The point being made is that angels are not intimidated by the three evil horsemen for, from their special vantage point in heaven, they see the whole scheme of Providence remaining intact.

**FURTHER
STUDY**

2 Kings
19:14-19,35-36;
Acts 27:21-26

1. How did an
angel help
Hezekiah?

2. How did
an angel
help Paul?

John observes four angels holding in check the four winds to prevent them blowing on the earth and causing great destruction. As he watches, another angel appears, crying out in a loud voice, 'Do not harm the land or the sea ... until we put a seal on the foreheads of the servants of our God' (v.3). The number of those who were sealed, John says, is 144,000. Bible scholars vary in their opinion as to who are the 144,000 and the 'great multitude' in verse 9, and the relationship between them. But it is quite clear who they are: God's servants, all of them, both Old Testament and New Testament alike. All God's believing people are sealed. The 144,000 (12 squared then multiplied by the cube of 10) need not be taken literally. Most numbers in Revelation are symbolic, and in this case the number signifies completeness.

What we are reading about here must be linked to the question at the end of the preceding chapter: 'Who can stand?' Well, for one thing, angels can stand. And for another, God's people can stand. When evil is unsealed, the Christian is sealed against it by the Holy Spirit. This sealing fortifies us against the unsealing.

**Father, I know that You are more than a match for evil. Nothing
can successfully work against Your purposes. I draw confidence
from this, dear Lord. Help me always to view things from this
perspective. In Jesus' name I pray. Amen.**

FOR READING & MEDITATION - REVELATION 7:9-17

'And they cried out in a loud voice: "Salvation belongs to our God,
who sits on the throne ..."' (v.10)

Before moving on we remind ourselves of the connection
between the 144,000 (v.4) and the 'great multitude'
(v.9). John *hears* the number of those who are sealed against
evil but when he *looks*, it is 'a great multitude that no-one
could count'. The 144,000 and the great multitude are one
and the same – all servants of God. Throughout Revelation
John uses poetic forms and language, and this repetition of
ideas was common in Hebrew poetry. It is designed to tease
our imagination into seeing that the hearts of all God's
servants in both the Old and New Testaments are sealed
against evil. Though evil may harm their bodies
it cannot harm their souls.

**FURTHER
STUDY**

2 Chron. 20:1-29

1. How did
Jehoshaphat
triumph?

2. What did
they do after
the battle?

The people John writes about are not only
sealed but exuberant. And why? Because they
know that evil cannot harm them spiritually.
Thus they sing. It seems to me a most wonderful
thing that the people of God can still sing in the
face of evil. There is a charming passage in a
book by Henry Adams entitled *Mont St Michael*
which describes a pompous theologian attacking
a brother who belonged to the Order of Assisi over
some of his simple beliefs. This is how the passage reads:
'When the theologian attacked the Brother by the usual
formal arrangement of syllogisms, the Brother, taking out
a flute from the folds of his robe, played his answer in
rustic melodies.' Music and song are sometimes the best
argument we can muster against the attacks of evil.

Notice also that the robes of the multitude had been
washed and made white in the blood of the Lamb. This
most precious imagery of being washed in Christ's blood
is being omitted from some modern hymn books but
thankfully not from the hymn book of heaven.

**Father, thank You that I can take my place among the great
multitude of those who have been cleansed by the blood of Your
Son. My soul is safe from evil because of His great sacrifice. I am
eternally grateful. Amen.**

'Reversed thunder'

FOR READING & MEDITATION - REVELATION 8:1-5

'Then the angel took the censer, filled it with fire from the altar, and hurled it on the earth ...' (v.5)

Now we come to the opening of the seventh seal, which also brings us to the next great theme of Revelation – the power of prevailing prayer. When the seventh seal is opened there is silence in heaven for the space of about half an hour. Why silence? In order to *hear* the prayers of God's people. We are about to see, as Tennyson put it, that 'more things are wrought in heaven and earth through prayer than this world dreams of'.

Then silence gives way to action. As John watches, an angel comes before the throne of God with a censer and

FURTHER STUDY

Acts 1:12-14; 2:1-4; 4:23-31

1. What marked the birth of the Church?

2. What happened when the disciples prayed?

mixes the prayers of God's people with incense, combines them with fire, and hurls the censer over the ramparts of heaven so that it falls to earth. When it reaches the earth there are peals of thunder, rumblings, flashes of lightning, and an earthquake. The prayers which had come up before God and had been purified and set on fire by God's Spirit return to earth with tremendous force. George Herbert had a beautiful phrase to describe this. He called it 'reversed thunder'.

This is a passage to which I often turn when I want to remind myself of the power of prayer.

I don't know if it is the same with you, but sometimes when I pray for the Church and the world I wonder if prayer makes much difference. How wonderfully reassuring it is to learn that prayer is heard, purified, and re-enters earth like 'reversed thunder'. Have faith to believe that the prayers you offer for the needs of the world are being heard and, after having been mixed with the fire of God's Spirit, fall back to earth. What an exciting concept: today, as every day, earth will be shaken spiritually by the prayers of God's people.

Father, I am so grateful for the reassurance that when I pray for the needs of the world You not only listen but take my words, mix them with the fire of Your Spirit and put them to work. Help me to intercede more. In Jesus' name. Amen.

The part prayer plays

'Then the seven angels who had the seven trumpets prepared to sound them.' (v.6)

Having seen in the half hour of silence how prayer is used by God in His work against evil, the seven angels who were standing before the throne and apparently waiting for their moment, prepare to sound their trumpets.

A trumpet is a symbol of proclamation. Over and over again in the Old Testament the trumpet was used to call people to battle or to proclaim a religious festival. Here the trumpets are sounded to herald what God does in answer to prayer, and also to alert us to our part in His purposes. Please don't be confused about this. God wants to enlist our prayers in resisting evil. He could work without us, but such is His esteem for His people that He wants to involve us in the struggle. Many years ago a Christian author by the name of Paul S. Rees wrote a book entitled, *Don't Sleep through the Revolution*. That, in effect, is what the trumpets are saying: be alert to the fact that you have a part to play through prayer in God's programme of discipline and redemption.

The first four trumpets, when sounded, initiate great disasters on the earth: a third of the earth is burned up, a huge burning mountain is thrown into the sea, a great star blazing like a torch falls from the sky, and the luminaries – sun, moon and stars – lose one third of their light. The trumpets sound out not just doom but warning. These judgments, like the plagues in Egypt (Exod. 7–12), are meant to illustrate God's wrath against sin and alert men and women to the fact that He is active. Many are so consumed with their lives on earth, that they ignore the broader picture. We, as God's praying people, have a part in bringing to others an awareness of their need of God.

FURTHER STUDY

Exod. 17:8-16; Josh. 6:1-20

1. How can prayer win battles?

2. What happened when priests sounded trumpets?

O Father, the more I see how prayer plays such a major part in Your universe, the more responsibility I feel to step up my prayer life. Help me to place a greater emphasis on prayer. In Jesus' name. Amen.

A new way of seeing

FOR READING & MEDITATION - REVELATION 8:13-9:12

'And out of the smoke locusts came down upon the earth and were given power like that of scorpions of the earth.' (9:3)

Before the sounding of the fifth trumpet an eagle is seen flying and calling out, 'Woe! Woe! Woe ...' (8:13). How strange that in the middle of the sounding of the seven trumpets the image of the eagle is thrust into John's vision. It is as if God, knowing the human tendency to make light of judgment, breaks into the sequence with something that throws us off our guard. Even more awesome images of judgment are to come which demand serious attention.

The fifth angel sounds his trumpet and precipitates a plague of terrifying locusts. A huge hole is opened up in the earth's surface and locusts start moving with a deafening noise, attacking not vegetation but people. They are armed like scorpions, shaped like horses, crowned like kings, have faces that resemble those of humans, hair like that of women, teeth like those of lions, and their bodies are covered in armour plating. Will such creatures plague the earth? I do not believe so. Here again our imagination is being stirred, and the image of the locusts – a recasting of Joel's locust prophecy (Joel 1-2) – is intended to show the terrible consequences of a life that resists the overtures of God's mercy. Only the repentant are saved from the devastation of sin's consequences.

FURTHER STUDY

Joel 1:1-20;
2:23-27

1. How should priests respond to disaster?

2. What was God's promise?

The introduction of the figure of the Apollyon (the destroyer called the angel of the Abyss, or bottomless pit) in verse 11 makes the picture even more nightmarish. Again I emphasise that these pictures are meant to send the adrenaline through our spiritual system and enable us to see truth through new eyes. A great deal that is found in Revelation is found also in other parts of the Bible, but here the story of judgment and redemption is made vivid, so that many might find salvation.

My Father and my God, I am seeing truth through new eyes. May more and more people open themselves to the advances of Your divine grace. I am so thankful that Your love has won my heart. All honour and glory be to Your worthy name. Amen.

FOR READING & MEDITATION - REVELATION 9:13-21

'The rest of mankind that were not killed by these plagues still did not repent ...' (v.20)

Though there is a seventh trumpet to be sounded, the sixth trumpet is the last to herald a warning for the inhabitants of earth. A voice comes from the altar saying: 'Release the four angels who are bound at the great river Euphrates' (v.14). Their task, we are told, is to kill a third of mankind. How do the four angels go about this task? They have at their disposal a cavalry of 200 million fire-breathing, snake-tailed, lion-headed horses. Once again this is not be taken literally (thankfully!), as the images are designed to stir us and call our imagination into play.

It is important to notice that the voice John hears at the sounding of the sixth trumpet comes from the 'altar'. This, as we saw, is where the Church's prayers are processed and fiery answers returned to earth. Trumpet number six, like the others, is sounding out the warning of God's wrath against sin in response to His people's prayers that evil should not go unpunished and that justice might prevail.

FURTHER STUDY

Jer. 35:12-17;
2 Pet. 3:11-18

1. What was God's complaint?

2. How should we live?

We are told in verse 20: 'The rest of mankind that were not killed by these plagues still did not repent.' They did not stop worshipping their idols, which could not see, hear or walk. Too many people today give their attention to things which cannot save them. And so they become like the idols they worship, blind and deaf to the workings of the Living God. C.S. Lewis put it well when he said: 'God whispers to us in our pleasures, speaks in our conscience, but shouts in our pains.'* If men and women will not hear the voice of God in their pains, what hope is there that they will listen to Him in the midst of their pleasures?

Father, I stand amazed at the grace that continues to woo men and women despite their resistance and stubborn commitment to independence. But with all my heart I cry, 'Continue speaking, dear Lord.' Many may yet respond. Amen.

A time for everything

FOR READING & MEDITATION - REVELATION 10:1-4

'Seal up what the seven thunders have said and do not write it down.' (v.4)

Thinking back, you will remember that before the opening of the seventh seal there was a pause. The same happens again between the blowing of the sixth and seventh trumpets. During this interlude John introduces another theme – the importance and power of godly witness. Encouragements are given throughout the New Testament to be bold in our witness, but here, in chapters 10 and 11, that same truth is presented in a way that once again stirs the imagination.

Imagine seeing a mighty angel descend from heaven whose face is like the sun, who is clothed in a cloud, crowned with a rainbow, and with legs that are like great columns of fire. When he shouts the heavens echo his words with seven thunders. In his hand he holds a small open scroll. Angels are often portrayed as fluffy, syrupy characters, but not so the apocalyptic angels. They are strong and powerful with, as one commentator puts it, 'hell in their nostrils and heaven in their eyes'. John is about to write down the words he hears but he is prevented by the angel.

Relating this vision to our witnessing, it shows that our responsibility to witness is always to be balanced by judgment of what to say and what not to say. Holding back is as much a part of Christian witness as bold proclamation. Jesus, on the Mount of Transfiguration, told His disciples, 'Don't tell anyone what you have seen, until the Son of Man has been raised from the dead' (Matt. 17:9). There are other occasions in the Gospels when Jesus also forbad people to tell what they had experienced. They needed to know a simple but important truth, namely that there is a time to speak and a time to keep silent.

FURTHER STUDY

Prov. 20:4;
Eccl. 3:1-8;
1 Chron. 12:32

1. Why is it important to understand seasons?

2. How can we be like the men of Issachar?

Father, You have taught me in Your Word that there is a time for everything. Help me in my personal witness not only to know what to say, but what not to say. In Jesus' name I ask it. Amen.

Celebratory Open Day
at **Pilgrim Hall**

Join us on Saturday 13 July as we rededicate the ministry of Pilgrim Hall to God, affirming its future as part of CWR

> *'Unless the LORD builds the house, its builders labour in vain'* **Psalm 127:1**

In 2012, CWR took ownership of the wonderful conferencing facility of Pilgrim Hall in East Sussex. This was an opportunity made possible by the grace of God, with many generous donations from supporters from all over the world allowing not only the continuance of the rich Christian heritage of the site, but also the further development of CWR's ministry.

Conferences, courses and events have been continuing at Pilgrim Hall, but we have set aside a day this year on which to thank God for His gracious provision, to celebrate this additional new centre and to rededicate the site for future ministry within the CWR family.

If you are able to join us on the afternoon of Saturday 13 July, we would love to see you.

Between 1pm and 5pm there will be an opportunity for prayer and thanksgiving, to hear of future plans and to tour the site and meet the staff over light refreshments.

This will be a free but ticketed event.
To book or for further information please visit
www.cwr.org.uk/phopenday
or call +44 (0)1825 840295.

Bitter sweet

FOR READING & MEDITATION - REVELATION 10:5-11

'Take it and eat it. It will turn your stomach sour, but in your mouth
it will be as sweet as honey.' (v.9)

The voice which had forbidden John to make known the
message of the seven thunders now commands him
to take the little scroll that was in the angel's hand and
eat it. The prophet Ezekiel had a similar experience (Ezek.
2:8–3:3). Eating a book suggests assimilating it, digesting
it, taking it all in. Before we can truly tell out the good
news of the gospel we must internalise it; it must become
part and parcel of us. If we fail to do this our witness
is nothing more than 'gossiping about God'. It is a very
graphic picture of someone who has absorbed the Word of
God into their spiritual system so that they can
share it naturally with others.

FURTHER STUDY

John 6:60-69;
1 Pet. 3:13-17

1. What were
the mixed
reactions to
Jesus' words?

2. How should
we always be
prepared?

John is told by the angel that when he eats the
scroll it will be bitter to his stomach but sweet to
his taste. Almost every child of God will know
this experience. The Word, when it enters our
mouth, is as honey to our taste, but so often,
when the word we share with others is resisted,
we feel in the pit of our stomach the sourness of
rejection. Jeremiah, you may remember, took hold
of God's words with great delight, but later, when
the people refused to accept what he had to say,
he cried, '… the word of the LORD has brought me
insult and reproach all day long' (Jer. 20:8).

The Word is sweet when it comes to us from God, but
when rejected by those we share it with it can turn to
bitterness inside us. It is not that we are bitter because of
the rejection, but we experience the bitterness that comes
with rejection. But whether it is rejected or not, the Word
must be shared. 'Prophesy again,' John is told. The work of
witness is powerful and vital.

**Father, Your Word tells me that perfect love casts out fear. May
Your love so permeate my life that it will overpower every fear
- particularly the fear of rejection. I ask this through Jesus'
name. Amen.**

FOR READING & MEDITATION - REVELATION 11:1

'Go and measure the temple of God and the altar, and count the worshippers there.' (v.1)

We come now to one of the most fascinating, challenging and puzzling chapters in the whole of the book of Revelation. It presents us with a picture of God's people being spiritually assured. When I was young there was a trend among some Christians to write after their name the letters 'M.A.' which stood for 'Mightily Assured'. This practice was somewhat deceptive and came into disrepute, but looked at from our present standpoint, every Christian is an 'M.A.' – someone who is 'Mightily Assured'. The image of the Temple being measured can be taken as the assurance that our work of witness does not go unnoticed or unappreciated.

John sees the Temple in Jerusalem and is told to measure it and count the worshippers there. We must remember that the Temple was by this time just a memory as it had been destroyed by the Romans in AD 70. In this vision the Temple – the 'measured' place – represents the community of God's people gathered together who enjoy the security of perfect order. In the Church the dimensions are specified. There is an order that is inviolate. Here we find clear lines and boundaries marked out against the world, the flesh, and the devil. We know what to pray for (I Tim. 2:1–8) and how to pray. We know how the Church is to be governed, how it is to evangelise, and how it should represent itself to the world. We are also given the guarantee that where two or three come together in Jesus' name, He will be in their midst (Matt. 18:20).

How wonderful that in the midst of our chaotic world there is a measured place to which God's people can retreat. There, as the old hymnwriter Richard C. Trench put it, 'We kneel, how weak; we rise, how full of power.'

FURTHER STUDY

2 Tim. 1:7-12;
Heb. 10:19-25

1. Of what was Paul mightily assured?

2. How can we approach God?

Father, how encouraging this is. In the midst of a chaotic world You have provided for me a measured place. May this image strengthen me so that I remain steadfast, unmovable, always giving myself fully to the work of the Lord. Amen.

The witnessing dynamic

FOR READING & MEDITATION - REVELATION 11:2-6

'And I will give power to my two witnesses, and they will prophesy for 1,260 days, clothed in sackcloth.' (v.3)

The community of Christians meeting to worship is protected by a holy order, but the 'outer court' it would seem is not. There holy things, and those who witness to them, are treated with contempt. To understand the impact of these words, consider how difficult it is to speak of the things of Christ in the workplace compared with discussing them in church.

Forgive the repetition but the point must be stressed: Revelation does not tell us how to make a cogent testimony to the faith, but strikes our minds with imaginative pictures. Two unnamed witnesses emerge in this passage, both wearing sackcloth to emphasise their mourning for the uncleanness of the people to whom they proclaimed their message. The astonishing things they are able to do (vv.5-6) suggest the two who witnessed to Christ's glory on the Mount of Transfiguration – Moses and Elijah. These two symbolise for us the witness of God's people throughout the ages; Moses was the lawgiver and Elijah the reformer. The law is the revelation of God's truth; reformation is the application of it.

FURTHER STUDY

Matt. 5:16;
Mark 16:14-20;
1 Pet. 2:11-12

1. How is witness confirmed?

2. How may unbelievers be convinced of our message?

The two witnesses prophesy with remarkable power for 1,260 days. They have power to shut up the sky so that it will not rain, turn the waters into blood, strike the earth with plagues, and stand up to the ruling powers of the day. What this seems to indicate is that the work of witness is backed by both heaven and earth. This telling image of the two witnesses draws our attention to the fact that knowing God's law and applying it to our daily lives is the dynamic behind all Christian witness. There can be no true witness if either knowledge or application is omitted.

My Father and my God, quietly something is being burned into me: the work of witnessing is one of Your highest priorities. Help me know Your law, apply it to my life, then share it with others. In Jesus' name. Amen.

A tide about to turn?

FOR READING & MEDITATION - REVELATION 11:7-12

'But after the three and a half days a breath of life from God
entered them ...' (v.11)

The two witnesses who, we said, can be viewed representing God's law and its application are suddenly attacked
by a beast which rises from the pit, overpowers them and
kills them. Their bodies lie exposed on the streets for a
period of three and a half days and are refused burial. There
appears to be great jubilation on the part of the inhabitants
of the earth as they see the two witnesses put to death.

Christians are not surprised, of course, by the fact that
witnessing comes to such an end. The world has a long
history of rejecting God's truth. Here in the West, ever since
the Enlightenment of the eighteenth century, men
and women, generally speaking, have rejoiced
as they have sought to replace God's truth with
human reasoning. The conclusion of the past
centuries has been in effect: 'Moses and Elijah
are dead ... no longer will we be reminded of the
need to toe the line spiritually and morally.' We
live now in an age when much of the world takes
the view that there is no such thing as objective
truth. People argue, 'My truth is as good as your
truth.' Many celebrate, in effect, the dethronement
of truth and the enthronement of reason.

**FURTHER
STUDY**

2 Chron. 7:11-16;
Ezek. 37:1-14

1. How may
revival start?

2. Why should
we never
despair?

Is this then the way of the future? Not necessarily. Look
at the two witnesses once more. Though dead they come to
life again (v.11), and before the seventh trumpet is blown,
they disappear in a cloud as Moses and Elijah did during
the Transfiguration (Matt. 17:5). All this symbolises the
work of Christian witness throughout the ages. At times
it appears to have been overpowered and brought down
to death, but always it rises again by way of revival or
reformation. Such a time, I believe, is beginning as I write.
Revival is on the way.

**O God, grant that this may be so. Turn the tide of spiritual
oppression and rejection of Your Word by an outpouring from on
high that will revive Your Church and bring a powerful witness to
the world. In Jesus' name I ask it. Amen.**

Longsuffering mercy

FOR READING & MEDITATION - REVELATION 11:13-14

'Seven thousand people were killed in the earthquake...
the survivors were terrified and gave glory to ... God ...' (v.13)

O ver the past few days we have observed how the work of witness takes place in the interlude between the blowing of the sixth and seventh trumpets. It is as if the Spirit breaks in and interrupts the proceedings to assure Christians they are not forgotten, nor deprived of the presence and power of the Lord. We must not overlook the fact that the messages these trumpets heralded were given in answer to the prayers of God's people for justice and truth, and the desire to bring people to repentance. As the two witnesses are being caught up to heaven, a severe earthquake causes great fear to fall on the people of the earth.

FURTHER STUDY

Exod. 8:5-15;
Dan. 4:24-37

1. What was Pharaoh's attitude?

2. How much time did God give the king to repent?

Before we look at what follows the sounding of the seventh trumpet, it might be helpful to remind ourselves that the first six trumpets are sounded to alert the world to the judgment of God. Those who have still not turned to God will face the third woe introduced by the seventh trumpet. Trumpets one to four demonstrate God's power over the world that men and women inhabit. Trumpets five to seven reveal what will happen to those who do not respond to God's call to salvation.

John's vision of the seven trumpets reveals a God of justice, One who cannot co-exist with evil, but, I think more importantly, it reveals too a God of great mercy. This is not a vindictive God who delights to rain terror on a helpless people; He is a God who mourns over the sinfulness of those He has created, and gives them every opportunity to turn from the evil that has engulfed them and cling instead to Him, finding rescue and restoration. Those who want to know Him – really want to know Him – will find Him.

O Father, how good You are to the men and women of this world. In longsuffering mercy, not willing that any should be separated from You, You continue to speak. All honour and glory be to Your wonderful name. Amen.

Thy kingdom come

'The kingdom of the world has become the kingdom of our Lord and of his Christ ...' (v.15)

The sounding of the seventh trumpet presents us with a picture of the final and overwhelming display of the majesty of God. Some suggest that this is the fulfilment of Psalm 2, when God gives His Son the nations and the kingdom of this world will become the kingdom of our Lord and His Christ. The 24 elders fall on their faces before God and raise their voices in thanksgiving and praise. Those of us who pray 'Thy kingdom come' will one day see our prayers answered. The kingdom comes in answer to the prayers of the Church. We must never forget that. Our praying has more influence in the world than we will ever realise here on earth.

We know that this is speaking of the coming of Jesus because of the phrase 'who is and who was' (v.17). In other parts of Revelation, Jesus is referred to as the One 'who is, and who was, and who *is to come*' (1:4; 4:8, italics mine). Now the One who is to come has come. The song of the 24 elders shows that ultimately God's character will be found to be true and that none of the redeemed will be able to say that God is not just.

These verses mark the climax of the first half of Revelation. John's vision will continue to unfold, as he sees more of what it means when Jesus' rule and reign is established. For now, we are left with the wonderful promise that one day all that is wrong in creation will be put right. The popular view of heaven being a happy place we go to when we die, falls short of the full truth that will one day be a reality. God is the Creator of the whole world, and His purpose is to reclaim all that is His and make it all that He intended it to be – perfect in His Presence.

FURTHER STUDY

Luke 11:1-13; James 5:13-18

1. What did Jesus teach about prayer?

2. How was Elijah just like us?

Father, I pray again, as I have prayed many times before – Thy kingdom come. I look forward with anticipation to the day when You will reclaim all that is rightfully Yours and make all as it should be. In Jesus' name I pray. Amen.

War in heaven

FOR READING & MEDITATION - REVELATION 11:19-12:12

'She was pregnant and cried out in pain as she was about to give birth.' (12:2)

The changes of scene in Revelation can be confusing as one moment we are looking at the end of all things and the next we are plunged back into another phase of time. Through a rift in the temple of God John sees the ark of the covenant – the symbol of God's presence and faithfulness to His people. This sighting is accompanied by lightning flashes, thunder and an earthquake, interpreted elsewhere in Scripture as signs that God is resident in heaven and active. All this provides the setting for the next theme of Revelation – the clash between the kingdoms of earth and the kingdom of God.

FURTHER STUDY

Dan. 10:1-14; Luke 2:1-14

1. What opposition did the angel face?

2. What did the angel explain?

A pregnant woman appears and suddenly cries out in the pain of childbirth. At that moment a dragon with seven crowned heads comes into view, and is poised to devour the child emerging from the womb. The newborn child is male, and as soon as He arrives in the world He is snatched up to God. Following this John observes a war breaking out in heaven, when the dragon is dislodged and cast down to the earth. At this a loud voice is heard in the heavens announcing the dragon's defeat.

John reminds us that the woman and the dragon are not to be taken literally; they are 'signs'. Signs rich with meaning and symbolism that point to something else (12:1-2). But what? We are being carried back here to the beginning of the story of salvation – the Nativity. For what purpose? To enable us to grasp more clearly that the coming of Jesus to this world meant the beginning of the end for the dominion of our adversary, the devil. Some view this as an echo of the Nativity as seen from an eternal perspective: the birth of the baby in the manger was the birth of the One who would ultimately overturn evil.

Lord Jesus Christ, how blind this world is to the real reason for Your coming. How it must grieve You to see Your incarnation so misunderstood, so commercialised and sentimentalised. Forgive us and help us, dear Lord. Amen.

God Unannounced

In this extract from the book, Andy Peck introduces *God Unannounced* – a collection of Bible readings and stories from around the world to ignite your passion for revival

When Selwyn Hughes, the founder of CWR, was looking for a name for the charity that he was forming to support churches in the UK in 1965, he settled upon Crusade for World Revival. ... For many years he had offered his *Every Day with Jesus* Bible-reading notes free of charge providing the user promised to pray for revival in our land. ... Today the ministry is known by its initials CWR, but still values those roots.

... most would agree that revival has not come to these shores in the manner that Selwyn sought. ... In this book, six men who have written about or have a definite interest in revival provide us with insights from Scripture to stimulate our thinking, encourage our hearts and expand our vision for what God can do in our lives, our churches and our land. ...

Although there has been no widespread revival in the UK, God has been at work worldwide and I have tried to select a cross section that spans the globe. ... The stories are not designed to intimidate us, but create an expectation for God to move outside whatever box we may have placed Him in.

Order using the form at the back or online at
www.cwr.org.uk

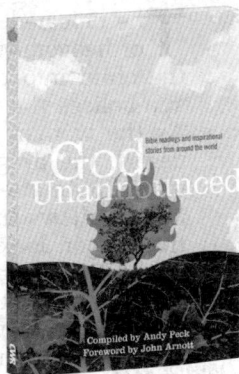

God Unannounced
Compiled by Andy Peck
Reader offer £5.99
saving £2.00 RRP normally £7.99

No room for pacifism

FOR READING & MEDITATION – REVELATION 12:13-17

'When the dragon saw that he had been hurled to the earth,
he pursued the woman ...' (v.13)

The defeated dragon (Satan), having been bounced out of heaven, turns his fury on the woman who brought the child into the world. Some suggest that the woman symbolises the nation of Israel from whom Christ came. As the woman is given two great wings to fly into the desert, the dragon pursues her and ejects a cataract of water in an attempt to drown her, but the earth opens up and swallows the water intended to engulf her. Thwarted, the dragon looks around for someone else to attack and goes off to make war against the rest of her offspring. We are left in no doubt as to who these offspring are:

FURTHER STUDY

Matt. 2:13-23;
2 Cor. 10:3-5;
Eph. 6:10-18

1. How did Mary and Jesus escape?

2. How can we stand against the devil?

'those who obey God's commandments and hold to the testimony of Jesus' (v.17). It is against the people of God that the devil mobilises his forces. As the devil is unable to attack Jesus he attacks those who faithfully follow His leading and call.

Some Christians I have come across don't believe in a personal devil. They need to know, however, that the devil believes in them. Christians are poised between two kingdoms – the kingdom of this world and the kingdom of God. Whether we like it or not we are involved in spiritual conflict. Whatever our view may be concerning pacifism in relation to the affairs of this world, there is no room for pacifism in the kingdom of God. Scripture tells us, 'For our struggle is not against flesh and blood, but ... against the powers of this dark world and against the spiritual forces of evil in the heavenly realms' (Eph. 6:12). Many Christians get no further than the first five words of that statement: 'For our struggle is not ...' We need not be alarmed by all this talk of struggle. Remember, He that is in us is greater than he who is in the world (see 1 John 4:4).

Heavenly Father, I accept that I am involved in a war, but I am thankful that the outcome is already settled. Help me play my part. In Jesus' name. Amen.

One Jesus

MON
10 JUN

FOR READING & MEDITATION - REVELATION 13:1-4
'And the dragon stood on the shore of the sea.' (v.1)

The picture of the deeply disappointed dragon standing on the seashore is meant to convey, I believe, a frustrated devil contemplating his failures. Obviously he needs another strategy. To wage war against 'those who obey God's commandments and hold to the testimony of Jesus' (12:17) a plan needs to be devised that will discourage them from obeying God and disillusion them about their Christian faith. Two beasts come from the underworld to assist him, one from the sea, the other from the land (13:11).

The beast that emerges from the sea is at first glance a fearsome-looking creature, but one commentator suggests that a closer look reveals it is nothing more than a patchwork job assembled from leftover parts of a leopard, a bear and a lion. The beast's seven heads and ten horns with ten crowns (a duplicate of the dragon) suggest that power is of the very essence to this creature. If there is one thing the devil lusts after more than any other thing, says Michael Wilcock, it is omnipotence.

FURTHER STUDY

Rom. 13:1-7;
Acts 4:13-20

1. What is our primary attitude to authority?

2. How might this be limited?

What we are seeing here in symbolic language is the anti-God state which derives its power from our adversary. For the Christians of John's day that meant the Roman Empire, but every succeeding generation knows its equivalent. Paul, in Romans 13:1, indicates that there is no authority except from God. God has ordained that the world should be run under a system of authority, but often the devil has undermined political systems and used them to intimidate and frustrate the followers of Jesus. Christians are called to uphold all that is right, and we must be careful that we are not swayed by patriotism to the degree that our eyes become blinded to reality. We serve another king and another kingdom, one Jesus.

Father, I pray for the politicians who govern my country. I recognise that politics is a field where Satan delights to roam. Help us to be aware of his tactics and combat him through powerful, persevering prayer. In Jesus' name. Amen.

Are you listening?

FOR READING & MEDITATION - REVELATION 13:5-9

'He who has an ear, let him hear.' (v.9)

The emergence of the beast from the sea is a striking image to draw our attention to political power struggles. Jesus came to establish a kingdom (the rule of God), and as Christians our first allegiance is to that kingdom. We are to obey the laws of the state (Rom. 13:1), but when they clash with the laws of God then we must remember we answer to a higher authority. One commentator says, 'If the devil's design is to separate our behaviour and our belief from the rule of God, politics will be a field in which he deploys his picked troops.'

FURTHER STUDY

Luke 2:49-52;
20:20-26;
Matt. 17:24-26

1. How did Jesus relate to the authority of His parents?

2. How did Jesus relate to authorities?

The beast, we are told, 'was given a mouth to utter proud words and blasphemies' (v.5). When a political system adopts the attitude 'I am God' and seeks to get its people to worship it as such then there can only be one word to describe it: idolatrous. Everyone has the right to discern, as Michael Wilcock puts it, 'between the state functioning *under* divine authority and acting illegitimately *as* divine authority'.

Forgive my returning to the section we looked at yesterday, but a comment is needed concerning the phrase which appeared in verse 3: 'One of the heads of the beast seemed to have had a fatal wound, but [it] had been healed'. Historians point out that the pattern of politics throughout history has been the death and resurrection of ideas. One ideology falls only to rise again. Christians must be careful that their interest in politics does not lead them to worship at its shrine. Our trust is to be in the blood of the Lamb, and we are to stay faithful to Him. It is so easy not to hear what we don't want to hear, hence John's use of our Lord's saying: 'He who has an ear, let him hear.' Are you listening?

Father, living as I am in an age when men and women appear to put more faith in a political system than they do in You, help me maintain my trust in You and in Your atoning blood. In Jesus' name. Amen.

FOR READING & MEDITATION - REVELATION 13:10-18

'He ... made the earth and its inhabitants worship the first
beast ...' (v.12)

The section before us now begins by pointing out that
the way of the beast is to kill off opposition; the way
of the followers of the Lamb is to endure it. The beast that
arose from the sea represents Satan's covert bid to get into
power politics; he seeks through this medium to interfere
with all that is right and just and true. The land beast,
however, is different. He looks like a lamb but has the voice
of a dragon. 'The beast from the sea,' says Michael Wilcock,
'is Satan's perversion of society; the beast from the land
is his perversion of Christianity.' Notice the Christlike
quality of the second beast; it is said to be 'like a
lamb'. However, it is an imitation of Christ and its
speech betrays its origin. It is a pernicious parody.

In today's world, as in the world of the first
few centuries, there are churches which put
nationalism before the kingdom of God. Any
church that encourages people to seek salvation
in a system rather than in the Saviour is not a
true church of Christ. Such churches may appear
to have God-given power, and their leaders may
seem to speak with authority, even demonstrating miracles.
'There is, in fact, no part of life,' warns one commentator,
'in which deceit is more prevalent than in religion.'

How do we protect ourselves from such charlatans? Once
again John puts his answer in an imaginative way: get its
number. The number he gives is 666. All kinds of theories
have been propounded as to the meaning of this number,
but for John and his first readers, it almost certainly
pointed to the Emperor Nero. Nero set himself up as *the*
authority, yet he was just a blasphemous copy of the real
thing. We must listen and learn from the One who has
true authority – Jesus.

**FURTHER
STUDY**

Matt. 7:15-23;
2 Cor. 11:1-15

1. What was
Jesus' warning?

2. What was
Paul's concern?

**O Father, enable me to look at all things through eyes that see
to the heart of issues. Help me discern the confidence tricksters
that pose as Your servants, and above all keep me faithful and
true to You. In Jesus' name. Amen.**

The power of worship

FOR READING & MEDITATION - REVELATION 14:1-5

'... before me was the Lamb, standing on Mount Zion, and with him 144,000 who had his name and his Father's name ...' (v.1)

We have been reading how the dragon, the sea beast and the land beast form a destructive trinity that infiltrates the political world in order to vie against the kingdom of God, and deflect our worship from the One we cannot see to the things we can see. This invasion might be alarming but it is not invincible. The dragon was overcome by Michael and his angels, the sea beast can be countered and the land beast seen for what he is. This destructive trinity is matched by three visions revealing the great drama of God being played out behind the scenes.

FURTHER STUDY

2 Chron. 5:11-14; Heb. 13:9-16

1. What happened when the Levites worshipped?

2. How can we sacrifice to God?

The first vision is that of the Lamb leading worship. The 144,000 referred to here represent the Church. We have already referred to the symbolic nature of the numbers used in Revelation, so let it suffice to say the number is symbolic of *all* God's people. This vision of the Lamb leading worship depicts, in my opinion, one of the most exciting scenes in the whole of Revelation.

In a world where political ideologies clash with the interests of Christ's kingdom it might seem strange that Christians should consider their first focus the worship of God. Some would put work before worship, but that is the wrong order. The Lamb leads us into worship so that our work might be more profitable and effective. The best workers for the kingdom are those who know how to worship. Worship first, work second. Nothing happens in worship, some might think, but that is where they are wrong. From the worship of God we come refreshed, inspired, reinvigorated to do God's work in the world. 'Excessive activism,' says Charles Brutsch, 'is typical of those who do not live by grace.' Worship is not a waste of time; it is time best made use of.

O Father, help me make worship my highest priority and, even though the needs of the world are great, help me not to substitute work for it. Make me a worshipper first and a worker second. In Jesus' name. Amen.

The power of preaching

'Then I saw another angel flying in mid-air, and he had the eternal gospel to proclaim ...' (v.6)

Yesterday we saw that worship is one of our great spiritual support systems because it enables us to stay refreshed and strengthens us so that we can face the challenge of living in a fallen world. Another support system which Christians enjoy is that symbolised by the three flying angels. The word 'angel', as you know, means 'messenger', and the message conveyed here is threefold.

The first angel speaks of salvation by grace – 'the eternal gospel'. The second angel speaks of Babylon, an issue we will look at later. Here it is sufficient to say Babylon stands for a world system which is in rebellion against God. The third angel brings a powerful challenge and proclaims that those who identify with Babylon will share its fate. Just as the Lamb standing with the 144,000 on Mount Zion represented the support system of worship, so the flying angels represent the power of preaching and proclamation. After all, what is preaching? It was defined by one great Welsh preacher, Dr Cynddylan Jones, in this way: 'Preaching is the act in which the gospel of God is proclaimed, the downfall of all that resist Him is announced, and the call to repent is encouraged.'

FURTHER STUDY

Rom. 10:8-17; 2 Tim. 4:1-8

1. Why is preaching so important?

2. What was Paul's charge to Timothy?

In a world preoccupied with wars, treaties, alliances and scandals, the need for proclaiming God's Word is greater than ever. Some might think that with so much in the world demanding our attention, there is little time left for this. We must make time for it. As we face the future our need is not for clever talks on current events but a renaissance of clear Bible teaching that is accessible to all. Though we need to take note of what our politicians and statesmen are saying, our greater need is to hear regularly from God.

Father, thank You for the many faithful preachers You have set in Your Church who tell us what You have to say about what is happening, and remind us of Your eternal plans. May their number increase. Amen.

Divine pruning

FOR READING & MEDITATION - REVELATION 14:14-20

'... seated on the cloud was one "like a son of man" with a crown ...
on his head and a sharp sickle in his hand.' (v.14)

The third support which Christians enjoy in the midst of a fallen world in fast decline is that of having their lives pruned spiritually under the direction of the Divine Gardener. In the passage before us now we see 'one "like a son of man"' (the term can be taken to mean Christ – see Dan. 7:13) sending his angels to reap. The first reaps a harvest from the earth, the second comes out of the temple with a sharp sickle and is instructed by a third angel to gather grapes from the earth's vines. Although this picture relates to the end times (see Matt. 13:30,39), and the judgment of the ungodly, I want to take this word picture and relate it to the way in which God works to prune His people.

FURTHER STUDY

John 15:1-17;
Prov. 24:30-34;
Deut. 32:32

1. What is the point of pruning?

2. What happens to the vine not pruned?

How many of us, I wonder, realise that every day God is at work in our lives and circumstances seeking to deepen our devotion, improve our characters, and develop our love for and relationship with Him? 'Everything we do, no matter what we do, however common and little noticed our lives, is connected with the action of God and is seed that becomes either a harvest of holiness or a vintage of wrath,' says Eugene Petersen. This encourages me tremendously. God, Jesus and the Holy Spirit are at work guiding me in holy living, supervising my days, watching over me, prompting me, leading me, influencing me for good so that out of my life comes a crop of grapes that delights the palate of the Divine Gardener.

These three support systems may not seem dramatic when compared with the power of the dragon and his beasts, but they have kept the Church alive throughout the centuries, and ultimately will call forth the prevailing kingdom of God.

Father, how grateful I am that the Trinity seeks to guide my footsteps through the world and bring honour and glory to You out of all that goes on in my life. Blessed be Your name for ever. Amen.

The exodus

FOR READING & MEDITATION - REVELATION 15:1-4

'... and sang the song of Moses the servant of God and the song of the Lamb ...' (v.3)

So far in Revelation we have seen seven seals, seven trumpets, and, in chapters 12 to 14, seven visions. Now we come to the seven angels with their seven plagues. These plagues, poured forth from seven bowls, introduce us to the next theme of Revelation – divine judgment. The desire for God's loving justice is deeply embedded in God's people. Psalm 13 expresses it like this: 'How long, O LORD? Will you forget me for ever? ... How long will my enemy triumph over me?' (Psa. 13:1-2). Hurting people cry out for justice. And who can blame them? Justice is not always to be found on earth. What about heaven? That God is just can be deduced from the words found in verse 1: 'God's wrath is completed.' He dispenses justice with a full measure.

John observes 'those who had been victorious over the beast ... sang the song of Moses ... and the song of the Lamb' (vv.2-3). It is interesting that prior to the outpouring of God's judgment the scene once again is that of worship. Only in the context of worship can the affairs of God be understood. Angels prepare to dispense judgment while a congregation sings a hymn. But what a hymn!

Notice the words 'the song of Moses *and* the song of the Lamb'. Two songs of Moses are recorded in the Old Testament, the first in Exodus 15 and the second in Deuteronomy 32. The hymn in verses 3 and 4 chiefly echoes the first of these songs, in which the people rejoice because of the exodus from Egypt. But great though that was, there is an even greater exodus which Jesus spoke about to Moses and Elijah on the Mount of Transfiguration (Luke 9:31) – the deliverance of men and women such as you and me from the penalty and power of sin.

FURTHER STUDY

John 8:31-36; Col. 1:9-23

1. How are we slaves like the Israelites?

2. What Exodus journey have we made?

O Father, I praise You for the deliverance from Egypt, but I praise You even more for the deliverance You wrought for me at Calvary. Because of it I am saved from the penalty of sin, the power of sin and, one day, its presence. Amen.

A just God

FOR READING & MEDITATION - REVELATION 15:5-16:7

'After this I looked and in heaven the temple … was opened.' (15:5)

The temple that we saw opened in chapter 11 verse 19 comes once again into view. This time, however, it is filled with smoke symbolising the glory of God. From this place – the scene of awesome holiness – the seven angels, their bowls filled with God's wrath, leave to pour out God's justice. Some of these judgments are similar, you will notice, to the plagues that afflicted the ancient Egyptians.

The first angel pours forth from his bowl a plague of painful sores on those who have the mark of the beast. The second angel empties his bowl into the sea, whereupon it turns into blood. The third angel does the same to the rivers and springs of water and they too become blood. Once again I emphasise that a great deal of symbolism is being used here. Our imagination is being stirred to show us that God's judgments are directed against anything or anyone who prevents His people worshipping Him. This is why the judgments came on the Egyptians. The negotiations between Moses and Pharaoh had one theme – worship: 'Let my people go, so that they may hold a festival to me' (Exod. 5:1-3).

FURTHER STUDY

Gen. 18:20-33;
Rom. 3:19-26

1. How did Abraham appeal to God?

2. How has God demonstrated justice and mercy?

Notice the reference to the altar (16:7). Earlier we saw the saints crying out for vindication from the altar (8:3). A longing for justice has been placed inside us all. God's response at that time was to give a warning – He longs for people to turn to Him before it is too late. Now, however, there is no warning. This is crunch time; the final judgments are at hand. Soon all that is wrong will be put right. Whatever your situation today, be assured that God's perfect justice will prevail – what a wonderful hope we have.

Father, there are many reasons why I worship You and why You are worthy to be praised, not the least of them being Your perfect justice. I too join in the company of those who adore You for the perfection of Your character. Amen.

NEXT ISSUE

The Great I Am

The epic story of the Exodus is one that has been told and retold throughout the centuries.

The deliverance of the children of Israel from slavery in Egypt and their journey to the promised land, provides a dramatic illustration of a powerful God who loves, rescues and restores. This same God longs to work in your life today through Jesus, our great Rescuer.

Join us as we journey through the book of Exodus and discover:

- The God who hears our cries for help
- How obedience brings freedom
- That we don't have to be perfect before God can use us

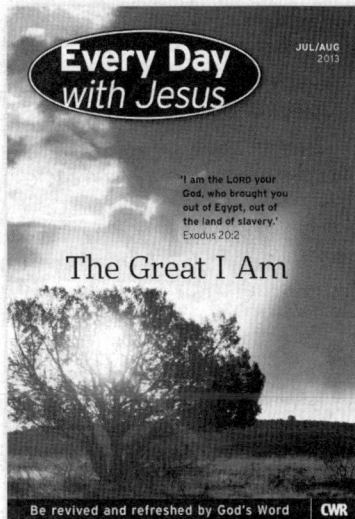

Every Day with Jesus

JUL/AUG 2013

'I am the LORD your God, who brought you out of Egypt, out of the land of slavery.'
Exodus 20:2

The Great I Am

Be revived and refreshed by God's Word **CWR**

Also available as ebook/ esubscription

OBTAIN YOUR COPY FROM
CWR, a Christian bookshop or National Distributor.
If you would like to take out a subscription, see the order form at the back of these notes.

Nothing can stop worship

FOR READING & MEDITATION - REVELATION 16:8-21

'The fourth angel poured out his bowl on the sun, and the sun was given power to scorch people with fire.' (v.8)

Today we look at what happens as the last of the seven angels pour out their bowls of wrath. The fourth angel empties his bowl over the sun and the sun is given power to scorch people. But those burned by the heat do not repent. The fifth angel pours out his bowl on the throne of the beast causing his kingdom to be plunged into darkness. Again the people do not repent.

The sixth angel pours out his bowl on the Euphrates and causes the river to dry up. Some see in the mention of the Euphrates in verse 12 and of Armageddon in verse 16 reference to a final battle when the nations in the northern part of the Middle East make their way to Israel. This is because Armageddon means 'hill of Meggido', a site a few miles southeast of Haifa. The seventh angel pours out his bowl into the air whereupon there is cosmic chaos.

FURTHER STUDY

Psa. 95:1-11;
96:1-13

1. How did the psalmist combine worship and warning?

2. Why does the Lord come?

As this battle is referred to again a little later, let me take you back to the vision of the worshipping congregation who provided the setting for the outpouring of these seven plagues (15:1-4). Judgment is inevitable on anyone or any system that interferes with divine worship. The greatest challenge that we face from the outside world is the prevention of our worship of God. The greatest deception we face inside the Church is the subversion of our worship. In many places around the world, the worship of God is suppressed and people face death if they refuse to deny their faith. In the Church, worship is relegated to a few short minutes of singing on a Sunday morning. Worship is such an important issue to God, and should also be to us.

Father, seeing what worship means to You I feel sad that so much of my time with You is spent in asking for things rather than adoring You for who You are. Help me worship You in spirit and in truth. Amen.

The great prostitute

'Come, I will show you the punishment of the great prostitute,
who sits on many waters.' (v.1)

Now we come to what one commentator describes as 'the plainest and the most obscure section of Revelation'. There is more clarity in the symbolic language used here than elsewhere, yet more mystery accompanies this section also. I draw your attention once again to the statement that with the seven angels and their seven plagues 'God's wrath is completed' (15:1). The completion of this judgment is seen in the overthrow of the woman on the beast, or the great prostitute as she is known here. Chapter 17 deals with her destruction, and chapter 18 is a song on the same subject. This sequence – story followed by song – is reminiscent of Exodus, and reinforces the thought that judgment is visited in order that worship may be better enacted.

John sees a woman dressed in costly clothing riding on a scarlet beast with seven heads and ten horns and covered with blasphemous names. A title is written on her forehead: 'Mystery, Babylon the Great ...' (v.5). A strange image, but once again one calculated to stir the imagination. 'If there are mysterious powers around,' it has been said, 'only exaggeration can help us see them.'

Babylon has been mentioned in two previous sections of Revelation (14:8; 16:19), but now we have a clear explanation. Babylon is the world. I am not talking about the world in a physical sense but in a spiritual sense – the system that seeks to set itself up independently of God. To flirt with the world is to live dangerously. 'Everything in the world,' says John in his first letter, ' – the cravings of sinful man, the lust of his eyes and the boasting of what he has and does – comes not from the Father but from the world' (1 John 2:16). We are to be in the world but not of it.

FURTHER STUDY

John 17:6-18;
1 John 2:12-17

1. How did Jesus pray for us?

2. How can we be in the world but not of it?

Heavenly Father, help me heed the warning You are bringing before me today. Give me the discernment and power I need to walk through the world without being of it. In Jesus' name I pray. Amen.

'The prince of this world'

FOR READING & MEDITATION - REVELATION 17:6-18

'I saw that the woman was drunk with the blood of the saints,
the blood of those who bore testimony to Jesus.' (v.6)

The writer Flannery O'Connor, when asked why she created such bizarre characters in her stories, replied that 'for the near-blind you have to draw very large simple caricatures'. The appearance of the great prostitute is more than a warning about sexual infidelity; the image is intended to open our eyes to the terrible influence of a godless world.

A prostitute takes men to bed not for the joining of souls but merely the joining of bodies. By such means both prostitute and client are demeaned and impoverished.

FURTHER STUDY

2 Cor. 4:1-6;
James 4:1-7

1. What has the god of this age done?

2. How should we relate to the world?

Prostitution says that love can be purchased and that sexuality is nothing more than appetite. The seven heads and ten horns are symbolic of destructive tendencies which we encounter in our everyday life. Everyone looks for meaning and purpose in life, and the great prostitute says, 'You can find it in me. Come to my bed ... there you will find meaning, purpose, love, everything your soul longs for.'

We must watch, of course, that we do not fall into the trap of thinking of the world as just an evil influence, for behind it is an evil intelligence. Jesus referred to the devil as 'the prince of this world' (John 14:30; 16:11). There is a deceiver at work in this world who seeks to attract people away from the worship of God to the worship of pleasure, sex, drugs, and so on. Every time I read this seventeenth chapter of Revelation the words of John from his first letter ring in my mind: 'Do not love the world or anything in the world ... The world and its desires pass away, but the man who does the will of God lives for ever' (1 John 2:15,17). I can understand why we need John's bizarre caricature. Without it we would not see things so clearly.

O Father, protect my soul from being invaded by the spirit of the world. I long to be like Your Son, who said, 'The prince of this world comes but finds no foothold in me.' I pray this in and through Jesus' precious name. Amen.

FOR READING & MEDITATION - REVELATION 18:1-24

'With a mighty voice he shouted: "Fallen! Fallen is Babylon the Great!"' (v.2)

At the beginning of chapter 17 we saw how one of the seven angels revealed to John the great prostitute. In this chapter (which we shall consider in one day's meditations) another angel comes from heaven with a glory that far outshines the colourfulness of the prostitute and announces her downfall. However attractive and appealing the spirit of the world may be, its downfall is sure. Its beguiling voice is no match for the compelling voice of the angel.

In verse 4 another angelic voice is heard issuing a warning to God's people not to be caught up in the spirit of the world, and this is then followed by another exposé of her evil deception. It is interesting to note that the longest laments over the demise of the great prostitute are uttered by the merchants and sea traders (vv.11-19). Through worshipping the great prostitute they gained everything their hearts were set on yet finished up with nothing. It was not just their business ventures that collapsed but their religion – a religion of self-interest.

FURTHER STUDY

Prov. 27:20;
1 Tim. 6:3-19

1. What are never satisfied?

2. What was Paul's warning?

Finally another angel is seen (v.21) who takes up a huge boulder and throws it into the sea, whereupon all becomes calm. The distinctive feature of this scene is that whereas previously all destruction has been accompanied by great noise, the end of Babylon, the great prostitute, occurs in stillness and silence. The music dies down, the sound of the workman's hammer is heard no more. No more bartering, no more trading, no more leisure, industry, no more noisy distractions. The enormous boulder, the size of a millstone, drops beneath the surface of the sea and it is as though Babylon had never been. There is a way that leads to life – and this is not it!

Heavenly Father, if I am ever tempted to join forces with the world help me to remember that it is going nowhere. May I be on my guard so that nothing draws me away from You. In Jesus' name I ask this. Amen.

Ringing hallelujahs

FOR READING & MEDITATION - REVELATION 19:1-10

'After this I heard what sounded like the roar of a great multitude in heaven shouting: "Hallelujah!"' (v.1)

In contrast to the stillness and silence of Babylon's downfall, this chapter opens with a tremendous roar of a great multitude shouting 'Hallelujah!' This is the first time the word 'Hallelujah' occurs in Revelation, and its timing is exactly right. Many commentators have pointed out that the four hallelujahs found in this section are not to be understood as arrogant rejoicing at the downfall of all that is not good or a sadistic gloating at seeing God's final justice, but as an act of praise and worship to the God whose ways are just and perfect.

FURTHER STUDY

Exod. 15:1-18;
Eph. 5:25-32

1. How can we identify with the song of Moses?

2. How will the Church appear to Christ?

The first hallelujah (v.1) celebrates the judgment that a just God visits on the great prostitute. The second (v.3) expresses gratitude for her eternal incineration. Her smoke, we are told, 'goes up for ever and ever'. The third hallelujah (v.4), prefaced by an 'Amen', is expressed by the 24 elders, and the fourth (v.6) is a tremendously powerful congregational response to the call for worship issued by a voice from the throne (v.5). The great multitude go on to shout that the wedding of the Lamb is about to take place when the Bridegroom will take His Bride and enter into an eternity of shared joy and love.

Having considered the last two depressing chapters which tell the story of the great prostitute, how reviving and refreshing it is to turn from her cheap and gaudy attire to focus on the fine linen, bright and clean, of the Bride's wedding garment (v.8). This is a dress she has not made herself. It has been given her to wear. By whom? By God Himself. What a wedding it will be when the Bride – the Church – is joined to the heavenly Bridegroom. We often hear the expression 'wedding of the year'. This will be the wedding of eternity.

My Father and my God, to be saved from sin and have a home in heaven is far more than I deserve. But to be wedded to Jesus is something I find almost mind-blowing. It seems too good to be true. But I know that it is true. Thank You. Amen.

We win!

FOR READING & MEDITATION - REVELATION 19:11-21

'I saw heaven standing open and there before me was a white horse, whose rider is called Faithful and True.' (v.11)

The theme of judgment comes to an end with chapter 19 verse 8 and another theme emerges in verse 9 – the end of all things. This section begins with the angel prompting John to write of the blessedness of those who are invited to the marriage supper of the Lamb. When John hears the voice of the angel he falls at his feet to worship him, but he is told not to. Though we may admire angels, we do not worship them. The statement which forms part of the angel's reply – 'the testimony of Jesus is the spirit of prophecy' (v.10) – is to be understood, I believe, as meaning that at the heart of all true prophecy is Jesus. All prophecy in some way has to do with Him.

Very quickly and dramatically we move from a wedding to a war, and we see once again Jesus riding on a white horse, victoriously robed, leading the armies of heaven into battle against the beast and the false prophet. When we compare Revelation 19:20 with 13:14 we can see that the false prophet is almost certainly the beast from the earth. The battle ends with these two enemies, who have caused so much havoc in the world, being thrown alive into the lake of burning sulphur, and those who followed them being destroyed by the victor's sword.

It is predicted from the early pages of the Bible that evil will ultimately be eliminated, and here we see its death throes. I am reminded of the story of a new Christian who became discouraged as he read in Genesis of the entrance of evil into the world. Quickly he turned to Revelation to see how it all ends. Coming to the passage before us today he breathed a sigh of relief and exclaimed, 'Thank God we win!' Keep hope; we do.

FURTHER STUDY

1 Cor. 9:24-25;
2 Tim. 4:6-8

1. What do we win?

2. Who will receive the prize?

Father, I am grateful that I am on the winning side. Your victory is my victory. May I walk through life conscious that though at times it appears some battles are being lost, the outcome is certain and secure. We win. Amen.

The thousand-year reign

FOR READING & MEDITATION - REVELATION 20:1-6

'And I saw an angel coming down out of heaven, having the key to the Abyss ...' (v.1)

Having seen yesterday the end of the beast and the false prophet in the lake of burning sulphur, the question arises: why was Satan not also consigned with them to the fiery lake? None of the speculations I have ever read makes much sense. It's probably another one of those questions best left until eternity.

In the passage before us today we see, however, that Satan is bound for a thousand years, during which the earth enjoys a period of peace and blessedness. This period of a thousand years is one of the most controversial aspects of God's revelation to John. Bible students are well aware that if you want to know how a person interprets the book of Revelation you simply ask them for their view of the thousand-year reign. Knowing this you will get a good idea of their approach to the rest of the book. Generally speaking people hold one of three views concerning this thousand-year reign. The first group is the pre-millennialists who believe that Jesus' coming takes place before the thousand-year reign. The second group is the post-millennialists who believe Christ's coming takes place after it. The third group is the a-millennialists who believe the thousand-year reign is not literal but symbolic. One thing we can all agree on, I think, is that the millennium has not yet arrived for chaos and destruction are alive and well and living on Planet Earth.

FURTHER STUDY

Luke 10:1-20;
Phil. 4:4

1. What did Jesus see?

2. Why should we rejoice?

No matter what our view of this thousand-year reign, every one of us can be encouraged by the knowledge that Satan and his evil influence will one day be suspended and then eliminated from the world. A friend of mine likes to call himself a pan-millennialist. 'Everything,' he says 'is going to pan out all right in the end.'

Loving heavenly Father, I rejoice that there is a horizon to Satan's history. You will allow nothing and no one to defeat Your purposes. I am in the hands of Someone who knows the end from the beginning, and for that I am deeply grateful. Amen.

The great white throne

FOR READING & MEDITATION - REVELATION 20:7-14

'When the thousand years are over, Satan will be released from his prison ...' (v.7)

John reveals that when the thousand-year reign is over, the devil will be released from his prison and allowed for a time to deceive the nations. The result of this will be the final battle of the ages, which has been referred to before as Armageddon. I must again emphasise that the various scenes in Revelation are not necessarily presented in chronological order. Some regard Gog and Magog as symbolic of all nations which resist God's rule, and the battle as an attack on the new Jerusalem, the focus of Christ's kingdom. Others believe Gog and Magog are people from the far north (see Ezek. 38–39), long-time enemies of Israel who are gathered for the final overthrow. The battle ends, however, with the defeat of the invading army, and Satan being consigned to the lake of burning sulphur.

FURTHER STUDY

Luke 13:1-5; John 3:14-21,36

1. What are our choices?

2. How has God helped our decision making?

Following this, John depicts for us what is sometimes referred to as the 'Great White Throne Judgment' when all humanity will be resurrected and brought before God for final sentencing. This final judgment will be made according to what is found in books containing the deeds, both good and bad, of all people, and a further book, the book of life, containing the names of those who trusted in the saving work of Christ.

The point being made here, I think, is that people are not sent to hell just because they have done bad things, but because they have not come to Jesus so that they might have life. God's great love and mercy are seen here again, as we realise that because the Father sent His Son to die for us, no matter what we have done in the past, our faith in Jesus secures our pardon.

Lord Jesus Christ, how glad I am that I have settled the question of my eternal destiny. I am in You and You are in me. Thus I am safe not only for time but for all eternity. I am deeply grateful. Amen.

What a prospect!

FOR READING & MEDITATION - REVELATION 21:1-8

'Then I saw a new heaven and a new earth, for the first heaven and
the first earth had passed away ...' (v.1)

John's final theme is heaven. And how it dazzles us. One
commentator describes this last part of Revelation in
this way: 'It is as if we have passed through a series of ...
rooms in each of which one window looks out on eternity
... and now we step out and find ourselves in the open air.'
There is to be, we are told, a new heaven and a new earth.
The Bible opens with the creation of heaven and earth and
ends with the creation of a new heaven and earth. Creation
is its first word and its last word.

**FURTHER
STUDY**

Isa. 65:17-25;
2 Pet. 3:12-13

1. How does
Isaiah see
the future?

2. What is
the nature of
the future?

The cataclysmic effects of sin have reached to the utmost
parts of the universe, but there is to be a cleansing
and a reconstruction based on our Saviour's work
on the cross. The phrase, 'there was no longer any
sea', is thought to refer to the swirling waters of
chaos mentioned in the opening verses of Genesis
and the fact that, once again, God has brought
order – and this time it is here to stay. Heaven is
not the end of all things but a new beginning. C.S.
Lewis, writing in *The Last Battle*, put it beautifully
when he said, 'All their life in this world and all
their adventures in Narnia had only been the
cover and the title page: now at last they were
beginning Chapter One of the Great Story which no one
on earth has read: which goes on for ever: in which every
chapter is better than the one before.'*

A city comes into John's view, 'prepared as a bride
beautifully dressed for her husband' (v.2). It might seem
strange that heaven is pictured as a city. However, the
underlying thought here is of a beautiful community
living in harmony and ready to receive God's love. Heaven
is a place open to all who trust in Christ. Can anything be
more exciting?

**My Father, I see that in heaven I am to be caught up in an eternal
story where 'every chapter will be better than the one before'.
There will be no more death, no more crying, no more sorrow, no
more pain. What a prospect. Thank You. Amen.**

The gates of pearl

FOR READING & MEDITATION - REVELATION 21:9-27

'The twelve gates were twelve pearls, each gate made of a single pearl.' (v.21)

We continue following John's wondrous description of future joy and blessing. There is some disagreement among Christians as to whether the New Jerusalem is an actual city or a symbolic representation of the Church in its eternal state. Either way it is breathtakingly exciting. We have seen already that here God dwells with His people (v.3), and the next thing John shows us is that the city is awash with light (v.11). God's first act of creation was to make light. It is light, too, that floods the new creation. A wall surrounds the city with 12 gates on which are written the names of the 12 tribes of Israel. Its 12 foundations, adorned with precious stones, have written on them the names of the 12 apostles.

It is difficult to select just one aspect of this description and explore its meaning, but the image that transfixes my mind is that found in the verse I have chosen as today's text: '... twelve gates ... each gate made of a single pearl'. A pearl, it has been discovered, is the product of pain. When the shell of the oyster is pierced by a microscopic worm or a speck of sand, immediately the resources of the tiny organism rush to the spot where the breach has been made. It then exudes a precious secretion in order to close the breach and save its life. If there had been no wound there would be no pearl. Pearls are healed wounds.

Can you catch sight of the rich symbolism of the gates of pearl? The entrance to the New Jerusalem is secured through the pain which Jesus endured for us on the cross of Calvary. Those wounds have become our healing. We cannot scale those jasper walls. We go in at a gate, and the gate is a pearl.

FURTHER STUDY

John 10:9; 12:23-33; 1 Pet. 2:21-25

1. How has Christ's pain caused beautiful fruitfulness?

2. How have we been healed?

Lord Jesus Christ, my Saviour and Redeemer, I see that in heaven there is to be an eternal reminder of Your sacrifice for me on Calvary. It is a truth I never want to stop thinking about, here and in eternity. Thank you, dear Master. Amen.

'Eternal nutrients'

FOR READING & MEDITATION - REVELATION 22:1-5

'... the Lord God will give them light. And they will reign for ever and ever.' (v.5)

Pictures and cameos from the Old Testament will have come to mind many times as we have gone through the chapters of this thrilling book. Here again the images recall those found in the Old Testament. The springing of the water of life from God's throne reminds us of Ezekiel's vision (Ezek. 47:1-9). Joel and Zechariah refer to it in their prophecies also (Joel 3:18; Zech. 14:8). This miraculous river, in fact, flows through the whole Bible and suggests abundance of life and fertility.

FURTHER STUDY

Psa. 92:1-15;
Jer. 17:7-8

1. Where do we flourish?

2. Why do we not need to fear hard times?

On either side of the river is the tree of life bearing all kinds of fruit, and yielding its fruit every month. This picture, I think, is intended to show that we will be dependent on God for our life in eternity in the same way that we are dependent upon Him now. The nutrients we need for our eternal existence will come from Him and not from our own resources. Our lives will be watered by the river of God and ripen into fruitfulness.

We will *serve* also. Heaven is not a place of everlasting repose. There will be activity – *joyous* activity, I imagine. And darkness also will be a thing of the past. No more dark nights of the soul. The Lord God Himself will be our light. One writer believes we will never truly see light until we see it in heaven. He puts it like this: 'The light of heaven is not the blur of a 40 watt bulb hanging naked in the night. It is *colours*, light that reveals the specific hue and texture of everything in creation. In that light we see not only objects but also their dazzling light-charged beauty.' Best of all, of course, our eyes will be focused on the Lamb. We may glance at each other but our gaze will be upon Him.

Father, the more I ponder the glories of heaven the more eager I am to go there. But all in good time. I have a work to do for You down here on earth. Let me not shirk the responsibilities of time because of my contemplation of eternity. Amen.

FOR READING & MEDITATION - REVELATION 22:6-11

'... let him who does right continue to do right; and let him who is holy continue to be holy.' (v.11)

As the vision comes to an end John falls at the feet of the revealing angel in an attitude of worship. This is the second time he has made this mistake, and the angel says, 'Do not do it!' I am a fellow-servant with you … Worship God!' (v.9). How sad it is when we become more caught up with the messenger than the message. This frequently happens in church life. Those who reveal the truth often become more popular than the revealed God.

Eugene Peterson suggests that some people treat the book of Revelation in the same way that John treated the revealing angel; they become so interested in what is happening that they forget God. 'They lose themselves,' he says, 'in symbol hunting, numbers, speculating with frenzied imaginations on times and seasons despite Jesus' severe stricture against it' (Acts 1:7). Nothing in Revelation is more explicit than the fact that the prophecy concerns Jesus and God. It is Christ's revelation we are to be taken up with, not the revelation of anti-Christ or the end of the world.

Along with the worship of God the angels command urgency: 'Do not seal up the words of the prophecy … because the time is near' (v.10). The urgency expressed in the opening verse of Revelation (1:1) is there also at the end. However blessed, encouraged and enlightened we are by reading these words 2,000 years after they were first written, we must not forget they had a special meaning and application for the churches of John's day. The book still speaks to us today, of course, and we are to use its message to help us continue to do right, to continue to be holy. That is its main purpose for us.

FURTHER STUDY

Mark 10:35-45;
Acts 1:1-8

1. What were the concerns of the disciples?

2. What was the concern of Jesus?

O Father, save me from becoming so preoccupied with dates and seasons that I miss out on the real meaning of all You are saying to me, namely that I must remain faithful and obedient to Jesus Christ. In His precious name I pray. Amen.

'Come, Lord Jesus'

'He who testifies to these things says, "Yes, I am coming soon."'
(v.20)

Revelation ends, as it begins, with Jesus Christ. He is the coming One, the Alpha and Omega, the Root and Offspring of David, the Bright and Morning Star. Twice in these last few verses Jesus reminds us that He is coming soon (vv.12,20). And for whom is He coming? Those whose robes have been washed; only they can enter through the pearly gates of the holy city.

But Jesus is not the only One who wishes us to keep before us the vision of His coming. The Spirit and the Bride also urge His arrival on the world's scene. They too say 'Come.' Those who have not tasted of the water of life and whose souls ache with thirst are urged to come to Him who one day will come to this world (v.17).

FURTHER STUDY

1 Thess. 4:13-18;
Jude 24-25

1. How can we be encouraged?

2. How will we appear before God?

We should close by considering the warning that anyone who takes away from this book or adds to it will be refused entrance to the holy city (v.19). If we believe that what God has said in this book is not sufficient and we make additions of our own, or if we believe its demands are not to be taken seriously, then we put ourselves at great risk spiritually. The safest position is to take God at His Word, trust in Jesus' sacrifice for us on Calvary, and wait with earnest expectation for His coming. There is not much time left.

The final statement is a promise of grace. Grace means strength, divine enabling. There is no better way of gaining strength for the days ahead than to ponder the truths in this book. How else could John finish his book than with the simple affirmation 'Amen', *Oh, Yes*?

Father, thank You for what You have shown me these past weeks of the glories of Your Son, my Saviour. Help me not to be taken up with times and seasons but with Him. I face the future with confidence knowing that all things are in His hands. Amen.

ORDER FORM

4 EASY WAYS TO ORDER:

1. Phone in your credit card order: **01252 784710** (Mon-Fri, 9.30am – 5pm)

2. Visit our Online Store at **www.cwr.org.uk/store**

3. Send this form together with your payment to:
   CWR, Waverley Abbey House, Waverley Lane, Farnham, Surrey GU9 8EP

4. Visit your local Christian bookshop

For a list of our National Distributors, who supply countries outside the UK, visit www.cwr.org.uk/distributors

YOUR DETAILS (REQUIRED FOR ORDERS AND DONATIONS)

Name:	CWR ID No. (if known):
Home Address:	
	Postcode:
Telephone No. (for queries):	Email:

PUBLICATIONS

TITLE	QTY	PRICE	TOTAL
		Total publications	

All CWR adult Bible-reading notes are also available in ebook and email subscription format.
Visit www.cwr.org.uk for further information.

UK p&p: up to £24.99 = **£2.99**; £25.00 and over = **FREE**

Elsewhere p&p: up to £10 = **£4.95**; £10.01 - £50 = **£6.95**; £50.01 - £99.99 = **£10**; £100 and over = **£30**

Please allow 14 days for delivery	Total publications and p&p **A**	

SUBSCRIPTIONS* (NON DIRECT DEBIT)

	QTY	PRICE (INCLUDING P&P)			TOTAL
		UK	Europe	Elsewhere	
Every Day with Jesus (1yr, 6 issues)		£15.95	£19.95	Please contact	
Large Print *Every Day with Jesus* (1yr, 6 issues)		£15.95	£19.95	nearest	
Inspiring Women Every Day (1yr, 6 issues)		£15.95	£19.95	National	
Life Every Day (Jeff Lucas) (1yr, 6 issues)		£15.95	£19.95	Distributor	
Cover to Cover Every Day (1yr, 6 issues)		£15.95	£19.95	or CWR direct	
Mettle: 14-18s (1yr, 3 issues)		£14.50	£16.60		
YP's: 11-15s (1yr, 6 issues)		£15.95	£19.95		
Topz: 7-11s (1yr, 6 issues)		£15.95	£19.95		
Total Subscriptions (Subscription prices already include postage and packing) **B**					

Please circle which bimonthly issue you would like your subscription to commence from:
Jan/Feb Mar/Apr May/Jun Jul/Aug Sep/Oct Nov/Dec

* Only use this section for subscriptions paid for by credit/debit card or cheque. For Direct Debit subscriptions see overleaf.

CONTINUED OVERLEAF >>

PAYMENT DETAILS

☐ I enclose a cheque/PO made payable to CWR for the amount of: £ _____

☐ Please charge my credit/debit card.

Cardholder's name (in BLOCK CAPITALS) _____

Card No. ⬚⬚⬚⬚ ⬚⬚⬚⬚ ⬚⬚⬚⬚ ⬚⬚⬚⬚ ⬚⬚⬚⬚

Expires end ⬚⬚⬚⬚   Security Code ⬚⬚⬚⬚

GIFT TO CWR   ☐ Please send me an acknowledgement of my gift   **C** ⬚⬚⬚⬚

GIFT AID (YOUR HOME ADDRESS REQUIRED, SEE OVERLEAF)

giftaid it

I am a UK taxpayer and want CWR to reclaim the tax on all my donations for the four years prior to this year **and on** all donations I make from the date of this Gift Aid declaration until further notice.*

Taxpayer's Full Name (in BLOCK CAPITALS) _____

Signature _____ **Date** _____

*I understand I must pay an amount of Income/Capital Gains Tax at least equal to the tax the charity reclaims in the tax year.

GRAND TOTAL (Total of A, B, & C) ⬚⬚⬚⬚

SUBSCRIPTIONS BY DIRECT DEBIT (UK BANK ACCOUNT HOLDERS ONLY)

Subscriptions cost £15.95 (except *Mettle*: £14.50) for one year for delivery within the UK. Please tick relevant boxes and fill in the form b

☐ *Every Day with Jesus* (1yr, 6 issues)
☐ Large Print *Every Day with Jesus* (1yr, 6 issues)
☐ *Inspiring Women Every Day* (1yr, 6 issues)
☐ *Life Every Day* (Jeff Lucas) (1yr, 6 issues)

☐ *Cover to Cover Every Day* (1yr, 6 issues)
☐ *Mettle*: 14-18s (1yr, 3 issues)
☐ *YP's*: 11-15s (1yr, 6 issues)
☐ *Topz*: 7-11s (1yr, 6 issues)

Issue to commence fr
☐ Jan/Feb ☐ Jul/Aug
☐ Mar/Apr ☐ Sep/Oct
☐ May/Jun ☐ Nov/Dec

CWR

Instruction to your Bank or Building Society to pay by Direct Debit

DIREC Debi

Please fill in the form and send to: CWR, Waverley Abbey House, Waverley Lane, Farnham, Surrey GU9 8EP

Name and full postal address of your Bank or Building Society

To: The Manager _____ Bank/Building Society

Address _____

Postcode _____

Name(s) of Account Holder(s)
_____

Branch Sort Code
⬚⬚ ⬚⬚ ⬚⬚

Bank/Building Society account number
⬚⬚⬚⬚⬚⬚⬚⬚

Originator's Identification Number

| 4 | 2 | 0 | 4 | 8 | 7 |

Reference
⬚⬚⬚⬚⬚⬚⬚⬚⬚⬚⬚⬚⬚⬚⬚⬚⬚⬚

Instruction to your Bank or Building Society

Please pay CWR Direct Debits from the account detailed in this Instruction sul to the safeguards assured by the Direct Debit Guarantee.

I understand that this instruction may remain with CWR and, if so, details will b passed electronically to my Bank/Building Society.

Signature(s)
_____

Date _____

Banks and Building Societies may not accept Direct Debit Instructions for some types of account